Verbs in Action
Blow Out

Dana Meachen Rau

Marshall Cavendish
Benchmark
New York

Happy birthday! You blow up
balloons. You blow out the
candles.

You blow horns and noisemakers.
It is party time!

You can blow air out of your nose and mouth. This is part of *breathing*. Breathing is moving air in and out of your body. Your body needs air to live.

Have you ever had a cold? Sometimes your nose gets stuffy. You blow your nose so you can breathe easily again.

Some musical *instruments* need air to work. Trumpets are loud.

Flutes are soft. Musicians blow air through these instruments to make music.

You can even make music without an instrument. Blowing out air through your lips makes a whistling sound.

A whale blows out air, too. It comes to the surface of the water to breathe. It has a *blowhole* on its head. The whale shoots air out of its blowhole.

Sometimes hot water blows out of the ground. A *geyser* can shoot water high into the air.

A volcano blows out hot air and rock.

You cannot see wind. But you can see what it blows. Wind blows the pinwheel in the garden.

When wind blows hard, it can be dangerous. *Hurricanes* are storms with very strong winds.

These winds can blow down trees and houses.

Why are dandelions growing all over the lawn? The wind blew the flower's seeds onto the grass.

Wind can change the way land looks. Wind blows sand to make a *dune* in the desert or by the beach.

Wind blows snow into *drifts*.

Machines can blow, too. On a hot day, a fan blows air to cool you down.

You may use a blow-dryer to
dry your wet hair.

You can blow your mom a kiss
when you leave for school.

If you get very mad, you might "blow your top."

Blowing means to move air.

Blow into the bubble stick. The air from your body fills the bubbles. Then the wind blows the bubbles across the sky.

Challenge Words

blowhole—The hole on a whale's head that it uses to breathe.

breathing (BREETH-ing)—Moving air in and out of your body.

drifts—Hills of snow.

dune (DOON)—A hill of sand.

geyser (GUY-zuhr)—Hot water that shoots out from under the ground.

hurricanes (HUR-i-kanes)—Storms with very strong and dangerous winds.

instruments (IN-struh-muhnts)—Tools used to make music.

Index

Page numbers in **boldface** are illustrations.

With thanks to Nanci Vargus, Ed.D.
and Beth Walker Gambro, reading consultants

Marshall Cavendish Benchmark
Marshall Cavendish
99 White Plains Road
Tarrytown, New York 10591-9001
www.marshallcavendish.us

Library of Congress Cataloging-in-Publication Data

Rau, Dana Meachen, 1971-
Blow out / by Dana Meachen Rau.
p. cm. — (Bookworms. Verbs in action)
Summary: "Discusses the action described by a verb, while making connections between people and
other living and nonliving objects. It also talks about other uses of the word in commonly used phrases."
—Provided by publisher.
Includes index.
ISBN-13: 978-0-7614-2288-4
ISBN-10: 0-7614-2288-9
1. Blow (The English word)—Juvenile literature. 2. English
language—Verb—Juvenile literature. I. Title. II. Series.
PE1317.B58R38 2006
428.1—dc22
2005026784

Photo Research by Anne Burns Images

Cover Photo by Corbis/Pat Doyle

The photographs in this book are used with permission and through the courtesy of:
Jay Mallin: pp. 1, 26. Corbis: p. 2 Grace/zefa; p. 3 Ariel Skelley; p. 7 Star/zefa; p. 8 Pat Doyle; p. 9 Virgo/zefa;
p. 13 Jan Butchofsky-Houser; p. 14 Frans Lemmens/zefa; p. 15 Corbis; p. 17 Jolanda Cats & Hans Withfoos/zefa;
p. 18 Andrew Winning/Reuters; p. 19 Jason Reed/Reuters; p. 20 Roland Gerth/zefa; p. 22 Sergio Pitamitz;
p. 23 Jeff Curtes; p. 24 Tom Stewart; p. 25 Roger Ressmeyer; p. 27 Joson/zefa; p. 29 Phillip James Corwin.
SuperStock: p. 4 Stockbyte. Index Stock Imagery, Inc.: p. 10 Henryk T. Kaiser

Printed in Malaysia
1 3 5 6 4 2

"dates" without the children introduced intimacy and spontaneity into their relationship. Their regular participation in musical and theatrical presentations, seminars, and workshops reawakened in him his repressed aesthetic sensibilities.

For the Record

Isaac's children were astonished by the changes. Their dad was no longer dismissive of their feelings and foibles. Their input into family discussions was welcomed and their feelings validated. The family dynamic had changed completely.

LINDA'S STORY

Linda came to see me for help with her disorganized and impetuous ways of being. Her parents were nonconforming holdovers from the flower-power generation of the 1960s. Doors were never closed, and privacy was not respected. All Linda's foibles had been indulged. Her whining about her repeated failures in arithmetic, math, and science convinced her parents that she would develop much better with homeschooling, with an emphasis on arts, music, theater, and dance. Linda quickly learned that she could succeed by complaining that she didn't want to be like other kids.

Her strategy was "artsy" nonconformism. Unfortunately for Linda, her parents died without leaving her an inheritance. She moved from job to job, place to place, home to home, and relationship to relationship. She was unsuccessful at selling her art and at theatrical and dance auditions. Her self-esteem hit rock bottom.

The Meaning of Linda's Story

Linda's cognitive *Sefirot* were clearly out of balance. Her *Chochmah* had become a shadow of itself. In addition, her neglect of her rational faculties had attenuated her *Binah*. Her impetuous

Repairing Isaac's Sefirot *of Cognition*

After working through a difficult completion process with his parents, Isaac committed himself to regular therapy. We tried the following interventions.

⊚ *Reparenting the Inner Child.* When I was dealing with my personal abandonment issues after my family's secret was revealed, my therapist suggested that I try reparenting my inner child. She told me to bring a photograph of myself as a little boy and put it on a pillow. I was to embrace the pillow and imagine that it was the little boy in the picture. I was to cuddle the little boy and tell him how much I loved him. I protested that I was far too rational to engage in such an absurd exercise. My therapist referred me to gestalt therapy literature, and asked me not to allow my overanalytical mind-set to block the healing process. We reached a compromise. I would not make a fool of myself by doing what she wanted in front of her, but I agreed to try it in the privacy of my own home. I was amazed at what happened. I soon got past the strangeness of imagining that the pillow I was cuddling was myself as a little boy. My tears began to flow as I acknowledged the boy's pain, loneliness, and fears, and reassured him that I loved him. Believe it or not, reparenting my own inner child had made me feel much better about myself, and had opened me to a world of feelings I had long disowned.

When my therapist saw the dramatic changes, she recommended that I read Hal Stone and Sidra Winkelman's work on voice dialogue. I recommend it to my readers.

I told this story of my inner child work to Isaac. His initial reaction was exactly the same as mine, but he agreed to set aside five minutes every day alone, and report what happened. Isaac's reparenting of his inner child had the same effect as mine. The rebalancing of his cognitive *Sefirot* had begun. He was now ready to become aware of his feelings and rid himself of his dysfunctional *Binah* activities.

⊚ *Role-Play.* By assuming the roles of his employers, employees, wife, children, and clients, with me "playing" Isaac in the dialogue, Isaac was able to experience the impact of his insensitive management style on others.

⊚ *The Empty Chair.* It was now no great leap for Isaac to experiment with this gestalt technique, this time in my office. He was able to imagine his inner child in the empty chair, dialogue with him, and, in time, encounter the disowned parts of his own personality. You can refresh your memory about the empty chair technique by reviewing page 166.

⊚ *Emotional Journaling.* After Isaac had read David D. Burns and Aaron Beck's *Feeling Good,* I asked him to pay attention to even the least sign of emotion and to record his feelings in a daily journal, in columns, under the headings *Time, Emotion, Trigger,* and *Response.* Here are some examples from Isaac's feeling journal.

Emotion: Fear. *Trigger:* His wife's threat to leave him following a major blowup. *Response:* Buying his wife a new convertible to divert her from her anger.

Emotion: Feelings of loss. *Trigger:* Seeing another couple in excited and loving communication about unimportant little things. *Response:* Unsuccessful attempt to engage his wife in the same kind of conversation.

Emotion: Panic. *Trigger:* Warning by his corporate directors that he was responsible for their profit downturn. *Response:* Failed attempts to strategize effective business alternatives.

Emotion: Depression. *Trigger:* Evidence of the disintegration of his world. *Reaction:* Self-pity and hopelessness.

Isaac was learning to tune in to his heart and accept the limitations of his usual rational, linear strategies for success.

He did not do the exercises in Burns's *7[   ] Handbook,* because we were reviewing his en[   ] ing in session on a regular basis. However, [   ] this handbook to readers who would like to [   ] journaling on their own.

⊚ *Systematic Desensitization.* Behavior modi[   ] Joseph Wolpe *(The Practice of Behavior Th[   ]* that it is difficult to experience positive and [   ] simultaneously. He trained his patients to r[   ] put themselves in a place of tranquillity and [   ] then asked them to list the things that sca[   ] starting with their smallest fear and moving [   ] to the scariest. While they were enjoying the[   ] relaxation, often with a soothing musical b[   ] instructed them to think over and over ag[   ] thing that was lowest on their anxiety list. [   ] long for this fear to be extinguished. They w[   ] to repeat the process, moving slowly upwar[   ] list of anxiety triggers. I asked Isaac to make h[   ] chy of fears and anxieties. Most of the items o[   ] taken from his feelings journal. His anxietie[   ] ally extinguished, and he was able to own his[   ] out fear.

⊚ *Couples Therapy.* In the safety of my office, Isa[   ] able to talk about her loneliness and the anger[   ] dren at Isaac's distant, "know-it-all," and auto[   ] family management. I asked Isaac to share wit[   ] feelings and fears he had recorded in his [   ] thought he would look foolish and weak, but[   ] prise, she was visibly moved by and delighted[   ] found vulnerability. Communication training [   ] deal with the difficult issues that had so long[   ] under the rug. Scheduling "surprises" and week[   ] moves from job to job and relationship to relationship, as well as her spending sprees when she had money, reflected dysfunctional *Da'at.*

Repairing Linda's Sefirot *of Cognition*

After her tearful completion at the graveside of her parents in Oregon, I suggested the following interventions, because she needed focus and structure.

- ◉ *Behavior Contracting.* I recommended an excellent summary on behavior contracting in *Behavior Therapy,* the classic work on behavior therapy by Masters, Burish, Hollon, and Rimm. Linda agreed to attend an accelerated evening high school completion program for six months. Simultaneously, she began work as an unlicensed teacher's assistant in a preschool program where her artistic skills would serve her well. Finally, she agreed to prepare a budget. She was to report on her adherence to the threefold contract on a weekly basis.
- ◉ *Systematic Desensitization.* This technique worked particularly well with Linda, because she had no trouble in identifying her fears, particularly in the areas of math, organization, and commitment.
- ◉ *Self-Esteem Training.* Linda recognized that her strategies had masked persistent doubts about her intellectual and social competence. I asked her to rebut the critical voices she was hearing with positive affirmations about herself. She was to list the best things her closest friend might say about her and give examples of these qualities. I suggested that she purchase Burns and Beck's *Feeling Good* and its companion volume, *The Feeling Good Workbook,* and I assigned her weekly exercises from the workbook.
- ◉ *Role-Play.* Linda responded to role-playing more rapidly than Isaac had. Given her interest in drama, dance, and the

stage, her imagination made role-playing the easiest part of her therapy program.

⊙ *Self-Forgiveness.* I asked Linda to catalog the things and relationships she had messed up. Next to each item, Linda was to note what it was that had made her feel guilty. We then discussed the philosophy and theology of repentance. This form of spiritual renewal is based on the conviction that mistakes can be forgiven, the past reversed, and demerits transformed into merits. The culmination of this intervention was to have Linda not only forgive herself for her errors, but to figure out how she could grow by learning from each of her missteps. Since Linda wished to deepen her understanding of the dynamics of forgiveness as a therapeutic tool, I recommended two more books, suggesting that she start with Eugene W. Kelly's *Spirituality and Religion in Counseling and Psychotherapy.* After she had read Kelly and asked for more, I referred her to Edward Shafranske's *Religion and the Clinical Practice of Psychology.*

REUVEN'S STORY

Reuven's career and personal life were hampered by procrastination and fear of commitment. His parents were strict in their religious observances. The life of the family revolved around the activities of the local congregation and yeshiva, and the rabbi was their primary source of information and inspiration. He frequently warned his congregation that God punished unacceptable behavior. Reuven's teachers at the yeshiva shared his rabbi's worldview, and forbade the children to watch television, threatening errant students with divine retribution. Reuven's parents were their rabbi's perfect disciples. Their primary strategy for family management was to threaten their children with the wrath of God. Reuven was convinced that love, divine and human, depended on impeccable conformity:

If you were not perfect, you would be punished. This approach kept him out of trouble at home and in elementary school, but after that, things began to fall apart. In high school and especially in college, he became a procrastinator. Ever convinced that his work could be improved, he did it over and over again, hoping that it would eventually be perfect. However, it was never perfect enough.

Ultimately, the very thought of handing in an imperfect piece of work paralyzed him, and he found excuses for putting off his assignments.

Reuven had also tried to find the perfect bride. He had been introduced to many women, but always managed to discover their flaws.

The Meaning of Reuven's Story

Reuven's cognitive *Sefirot* were out of balance. His procrastination reflected both *Binah* and *Da'at* dysfunction. Reuven had become trapped by his obsessive intellectualizing and could not decide when a piece of work was perfect enough to hand in. His fear of commitment also reflected a *Da'at* problem. He rejected prospective brides as imperfect, because he unconsciously knew that they would reject him when they learned of his imperfections.

Repairing Reuven's Sefirot of Cognition

During the follow-up sessions, we tried these interventions.

- ◉ *Completion.* Reuven's completion with his parents had been difficult. They were defensive and psychologically abusive, and he was concerned about violating the Fifth Commandment. Nevertheless, completion did finally occur in the form of a moving letter he composed and mailed to his parents.

◉ *Guilt Reduction.* The fundamental principle of cognitive restructuring is that feelings and behaviors are molded by what and how we think. Dr. Aaron Beck and his disciples have successfully treated reactive depression by having their patients modify their distorted thinking. For the more scholarly of my readers, I recommend Beck's *Cognitive Therapy of Depression* and the *Comprehensive Handbook of Cognitive Therapy,* edited by Arthur Freeman, Karen M. Simon, Larry E. Beutler, and Hal Arkowitz. At first, Reuven resisted what he called "secular" therapy, because he had been taught that most mental health professionals, like Freud, were atheists. Fortunately, however, Beck had not been the first to come up with the technique of cognitive restructuring. Rabbi Schneur Zalman of Lyadi had long ago used the same technique. Given his background, Reuven was ready to go along with this "rabbinic" therapy. I asked him to journal his guilt feelings, record the trigger, state briefly why he felt guilty, and to examine whether his guilt made sense. In the follow-up sessions of the workshop, I went over his guilt journal with him and helped him recognize the irrational basis of his guilty feelings.

◉ *Procrastination Reduction.* I asked Reuven to do the following exercise.

1. Identify one activity that he kept postponing.
2. List the advantages of postponing it (e.g.: It seems easier not to do it. I can do something else that I enjoy more. Who wants to fail?).
3. List the disadvantages (e.g.: I feel disorganized. I feel incompetent. I feel guilty).
4. Do a cost-benefit analysis of the advantages of procrastinating versus the costs of procrastinating.
5. If the cost of procrastination exceeds the benefit (which is usually the case), divide the task into its component

elements. Make a plan, beginning with the easiest elements rather than the task as a whole. Reward compliance. Do the next easiest component and reward compliance, and so on until the task is accomplished.

6. Repeat the process with another task that has been put off.

⊙ *Self-Forgiveness.* Self-forgiveness training was an obvious intervention for a person with Reuven's religious upbringing and feelings of guilt. My strategy was to reframe the doctrine of repentance. Traditionally, God is at the center of the process. It is to him that we confess our sins and from him that we beg forgiveness. While affirming the traditional view of repentance, I added the dimension of self-forgiveness and proceeded as I had done with Linda.

⊙ *Self-Esteem Training.* I used the same approach with Reuven as I had with Linda.

SPIRITUAL INTERVENTIONS

How can all of us, despite our early experiences of disappointment and loss, stimulate our underdeveloped *Sefirot* of cognition? Rabbi Moses Cordovero shows the way. In *The Palm Tree of Deborah,* he provides us with a detailed manual for balancing our *Sefirot.*

> How should the human train himself to possess the quality of Wisdom *[Chochmah]*? Behold, the Supernal Wisdom, though it is hidden and exceedingly exalted, is spread over all creatures . . . Behold, Wisdom *[Chochmah]* has two faces. The higher face turns towards the Crown *[Keter]*. It does not gaze downward, but receives from above. The second face, the lower one, turns downward to control the *Sephiroth,* emanating all of its wisdom to them. So, too, the human should have two faces: the one, our solitude with our Creator, in order to add to our wisdom and to

perfect it; the other to teach others of the wisdom that the
Holy One, Blessed is he, has poured out upon us. (p. 80)

By "our solitude with our Creator," Rabbi Cordovero means meditation. In fact, the great Chasidic master Rabbi Nachman of Bratslav (1772–1811) called his meditation exercises *hitbodedut* (solitude
with God). Some of these are now available in English. I also recommend Rabbi Aryeh Kaplan's *Meditation and the Bible, Meditation and Kabbalah,* and *Jewish Meditation.*

Although Rabbi Cordovero does not give us the details of his
Chochmah meditation, others have done so, and their techniques
often involve brain-wave entrainment, since opening to intuition is
a function of theta brain-wave activity. Theta brain-wave meditation is an effective way of enhancing our *Chochmah.* Brain waves
are tiny electromagnetic waveforms that are produced by the activity of our brain cells. They can be measured by electroencephalo-
grams (EEGs) and are recorded in cycles per second, or hertz (Hz).
Our brain-wave frequencies respond to changes in consciousness.

There are four major brain-wave patterns. Beta brain waves
(30–13 Hz) are associated with linear, logical thinking. They are
present during ordinary wakeful states. In our society, these beta
wave patterns predominate. Alpha brain waves (13–8 Hz), which
are produced when the mind begins to move from external to
internal states of consciousness, are present when we close our eyes
or begin to fall asleep. Theta brain-wave patterns (8–3.5 Hz) can
be observed both during our dream states and when we experience
periods of wakeful creativity. Many delta brain waves (3.5–0.5 Hz)
are present when we are in deep sleep.

Since 1977, researchers have thrown increasing light on the
neurological changes that occur during meditation. The pioneering
work of Dr. Elmer Green of the Menninger Clinic in Topeka,

Kansas, demonstrated that we can consciously "turn on" our theta brain-wave sequences. He showed that when we do so, we can experience paranormal states of consciousness such as mental telepathy and clairvoyance. Dr. Green also showed that the heightened spiritual awareness of the yogi masters who participated in his laboratory experiments was associated with their steady, wakeful theta brain-wave patterns. Many of the college students who were subjects in his theta studies reported enhanced creativity and deepening and consistent intuition. Theta brain-wave activity in sleep states thus explains the prophetic nature of some dreams.

In the decades since Elmer Green's groundbreaking findings were published, there were sporadic attempts to study brain activity in meditators and years of tests with monks and yogis in Western laboratories. However, it was not till the turn of the century that an experiment was conducted to assess meditation as mind training using an exceptionally advanced meditator, functional magnetic resonance imaging (fMRI), and other sophisticated instruments. In *Destructive Emotions,* Daniel Goleman describes the functional MRI as the "current gold standard of research on the brain's role in behavior" (p. 7). Going beyond the conventional MRI, which simply reveals the brain's structures, the fMRI records how zones of the brain change their level of activity from moment to moment. FMRI studies had previously revealed that many brain areas are recruited into synchrony when we perceive, think, or feel. What would the fMRI reveal about the brain activity of a very advanced meditator in "open state meditation, a thought-free wakefulness where the mind is open, vast, and aware, with no intentional mental activity" (p. 8), focused on nothing?

The experiment took place in the E. M. Keck Laboratory for Functional Brain Imaging and Behavior at the University of Wisconsin in Madison, following the eighth round of colloquiums of neuroscientists, psychologists, philosophers, and Buddhist scholars of the Mind and Life Institute, located in Boulder, Colorado. Richard Davidson, the director of the Laboratory for Affective Neuroscience at the university, and his colleagues, both at the university and in the Mind and Life Institute, had invited a meditator, far more experienced than the meditators in previous studies, to participate in this experiment. The fMRI revealed that his open-state meditation produced little neural synchrony across the brain, contrasting with other meditative modes and wakeful states that involved many other brain areas in synchrony. Simply put, the experiment revealed that this mode of meditation can all but "silence" the brain. In kabbalistic terms, Davidson's experiment showed that when *Binah, Da'at,* and the *Sefirot* of feeling are stilled, *Chochmah* becomes fully operational, open, aware, and unimpeded in its intuitive activities.

Davidson's findings are reinforced and further explained by the neurobiological model of the meditative experience proposed by radiologist Andrew Newberg and psychiatrist Eugene D'Aquili. In their *Why God Won't Go Away: Brain Science and the Biology of Belief,* which they coauthored with Vince Rause, Newberg and D'Aquili describe the experiments they conducted at about the same time as Davidson and his colleagues were using the fMRI technique. Their subjects were eight experienced Tibetan meditators and several Franciscan nuns at prayer. The investigators used single photon emission computed tomography (SPECT). The scan images showed unusual activity in the top rear section of their subjects' brains (the posterior superior parietal lobe) during peak periods of meditation or intensely religious moments of prayer. This part of the brain is responsible for orienting the individual in physical space, which it does by generating clear, consistent cognition of the physical limits of the self by drawing a "sharp distinction between the individual and everything else, to sort out the you from the infinite not-you that makes up the rest of the universe" (p. 5). Before meditation and intensely directed prayer, this area is the center of furious neurological activity, which appears as bursts of vivid red and yellow on the scan. However, at the peak of the meditative state or during intensely focused moments of prayer, the area is bathed in dark blotches of cool greens and blues, indicating a sharp reduction in the level of neurological activity. At these peak moments, practiced mystics and meditators enjoy altered states of consciousness that have been described either as the absorption of the self into something larger or the attachment of the self to the Infinite. In this state, "normal rational thought processes give way to more intuitive ways of understanding . . . [that are] intimations of the presence of the sacred or the holy" (p. 101). Earlier in the book, I described these states as *Chochmah* consciousness.

Newberg and D'Aquili describe the neurological mechanism for the experience of transcendence as follows: Meditation begins with the willed intention to clear the mind of all thought, perception, and emotions. Conscious intention is facilitated by the brain's right attention association area. The attention area, using the thalamus as its conduit, causes the limbic structure, called the hippocampus, to dampen the flow of neural input into many brain structures, including the area whose scan color changes during meditation I have described. The orientation area becomes increasingly deprived of information (deafferented). "As this blockage continues, bursts of neural impulses begin to travel, with increasing energy, from the deafferented orientation area, down through the limbic system to the ancient neural structure known as the hypothalamus" (p. 118), causing strong sensations of quiescence. This process discharges a burst of neural impulses back through the limbic system, ultimately reaching the attention association area. The attention association area now registers the calming impulses, relays them back down the circuit, facilitating a "reverberating circuit . . . in the brain, with a stream of neural impulses gathering strength and resonance as they race again and again along the neural speedway, fostering deeper and deeper levels of meditative calm with every pass" (p. 118).

Newberg and D'Aquili's laboratory findings and neurological model suggest that humans are hardwired for the experience of transcendence, and that the mystic state is not a function of the religious imagination but a neurological fact. This is why they coin the term *neurotheology* to describe their model.

Theta meditation is an accessible and easily mastered path to mystical contemplation. Dr. Jeffrey Thompson of the Center for Neuroacoustic Research in Encinitas, California, has made available a simple method for achieving the neurological changes that are associated with the experience of transcendence through brain-wave entrainment. He has found that the brain has a tendency to match its own wave impulses to those of exterior sound pulses, and has produced a number of CDs with special theta frequency pulses in the sound track. Although his recordings do not change the brain-wave patterns for long after you listen to them, they do have the cumulative effect of training the nervous system. The more you enter theta brain-wave consciousness, the easier it is for you to access it at will. For more information on his work and recordings, visit www.neuroacoustic.com. Thompson has created the music with its embedded theta frequency pulses for my meditation CD. See page 287 for details.

THETA MEDITATION FOR CHOCHMAH ACTIVATION

You can either record this meditation yourself or use the *Chochmah* meditation on my CD.

1. Remove jewelry and any tight clothing. If it is comfortable for you to do so, also take off your shoes.

2. Spend a few minutes doing exercises such as stretching and running in place.

3. Sit comfortably in your chair with your hands palms up, holding your back straight and away from the back of the chair. Keep your knees as close together as is comfortable.

4. Recite the following prayer: "Lord God, I invoke your blessings upon me as I open my *Chochmah* to your energy and light. I thank you for this opportunity of gaining access to my intuitive and creative potential. Help me and I shall be helped. So be it. Amen."

5. Breathe in through your nose and out through your mouth, with your head held upright and as far back as you can, and your back straight. Breathe this way fourteen times.

6. Be aware of your body. Remember that awareness is not the same as focus. Simply allow your mind to be aware of your body. Feel your feet touching the floor, your thighs on the chair, and your hands on your knees. Let this awareness spread to the rest of your body.

7. Be aware of the pulsations of energy moving from the base of your spine to your head. You may experience this *Nefesh* energy as a ray of light moving up and down your spine.

8. Be aware of your breath. Do not breathe deeply. Simply be aware of the air coming in and going out, and of the *Ru'ach* energies it contains.

9. Retain awareness of your body, the *Nefesh* vibrations and light pulsating up and down your spine, and the *Ru'ach* energies of your breath. Place your tongue on the roof of your mouth and be aware of the *Neshamah* center in your brain, above and a little to the right of where your tongue is touching your palate. Be aware of the sense of restfulness, tranquillity, and peace that you are experiencing in your *Neshamah* center. Be aware of how it is opening to the light and energy of *Havayah* that penetrate your skull and join you to the higher reaches of your soul and to the Self.

10. While retaining awareness of your body, the *Nefesh* energies pulsating in your spine, the *Ru'ach* energies in your breath,

and the peace and tranquillity of *Neshamah*, allow your awareness to expand to include the room in which you are sitting, the house, your block, your city, your state, your country, your continent, and the entire earth. Allow this awareness to expand to include our solar system, the galaxies, and all the universes hidden and revealed. Let go. Remain with this expanded awareness for a few moments.

11. Repeat the breathing exercise, inhaling fourteen times through your nose and exhaling through your mouth.

12. Repeat the expansion of awareness to include your body, the *Nefesh* energies of your spine, the *Ru'ach* energies of your breath, and the tranquillity and restfulness of the *Neshamah* energies in your brain. Expand your awareness to include your room, your house, your block, your country, your continent, the earth, the solar system, the galaxies, and all universes hidden and revealed. Let go. Remain in this state for a few minutes.

13. Repeat steps five through twelve. Let go.

14. Inhale deeply and slowly through your nose, with your head held back. Exhale deeply and slowly through your mouth. Repeat six times.

15. Once again, return to the *Nefesh* energies that are pulsating up and down your spine. Feel the vibrations. Picture the movement of the shaft of light up and down your spine. Be aware of your gentle breathing. Do not breathe deeply. While holding your awareness of the *Nefesh* energies, expand your awareness to the *Ru'ach* energies of your breath. Expand your awareness to the *Neshamah* center in your brain. Expand your awareness to include your room, your house, your block, your country, your continent, the earth, the solar system, the galaxies, and all universes hidden and revealed. Let go.

16. Picture the golden light of *Chochmah* energy entering through your forehead, filling your *Neshamah* center with light, tranquillity, and inspiration. Remain in this place of tranquillity, openness, and light for three or four minutes.

17. Allow the light of *Chochmah* to flow through all your *Sefirot*,

passing to your left-brain *Binah* center, the *Da'at* center in your throat, your *Chesed* center on the right side of your heart, your *Gevurah* center on the left side, your *Tif'eret* center in your diaphragm, your *Netzach* center on the lower right side of your body, your *Hod* center on the lower left side, the *Yesod* center where your organs of reproduction are located, and your *Malchut* center in your feet, where you are grounded to the earth.

18. Remain with the flow of *Chochmah* energy throughout your *Sefirot* for two or three minutes.

19. Raise your hands level with your chest, palms facing each other. Envision a small earth between your hands. Bless the good earth. Send your energy and your light to the earth through your body, down your legs, and into the earth. Feel yourself grounded once again.

20. Bless your family, your community, your fellow citizens, your people, and all humankind.

21. Recite the closing prayer: "Lord of the Universe, I thank you for the blessings of this experience. I thank you for opening my *Chochmah* to the light and energy of *Havayah*. I thank you for all your bounty, for the good earth, and all that is therein. I bless you, even as you have blessed me. I bless the earth, even as you have blessed it with *Havayah*. Amen and amen."

22. Sweep away the excess by holding your hands, palms outward, above your head and moving them down your sides rapidly in a sweeping motion, dispersing the energy behind you on your left and right sides. Repeat this sweeping motion several times. You may also sweep the energy by extending your left hand palm forward and sweeping it over your right shoulder. Do the same with your right hand. Repeat several times.

TIKKUN OF CHOCHMAH BY LEARNING AND TEACHING

In addition to meditation, the quotation from *The Palm Tree of Deborah* on pages 183–184 specifies learning and teaching as a way of achieving *tikkun* for *Chochmah*. The sages taught that one should set aside fixed times for the study of Torah. Participants in Torah classes are encouraged to ask questions, make suggestions, and share their insights, and in this way, students become teachers. Study dialogue is also an ancient Jewish learning strategy. One chooses a partner for the exploration of a classical text from the library of sacred literature. Points are clarified by dialogue and debate, and here, too, the lines between teaching and learning become blurred.

Most communities offer an abundance of learning and teaching opportunities. Set up at least one weekly learning commitment. Be prepared for the sense of wonder you will experience when those who study with you become excited by your insights. Enjoy the development and dissemination of the fruits of your *Chochmah*.

TIKKUN OF BINAH

I have taken some liberties with Rabbi Cordovero's *tikkun* of *Binah*. Strictly speaking, what I represent as *Binah* repair is part of Rabbi Cordovero's strategy for the *tikkun* of *Chesed*. However, his *tikkun* of *Chesed* is helpful to people with *Binah* imbalance, because those who cannot deal with feelings and are uncomfortable in authentic relationships often remain in their heads rather than in their hearts. This defense mechanism permits them distance. Dispassionate analysis, by definition, reflects noninvolvement. Furthermore, if people can win every argument and succeed in twisting facts to their advantage, they appear superior. There is nothing quite as good as one-upmanship for maintaining distance. Winning points in this way infuriates the other person and permits the mind game expert the satisfaction of saying, "She's emotional. Therefore, she loses her cool. I'm rational. Therefore, I'm always in control of myself and the situation." This type of inner dialogue

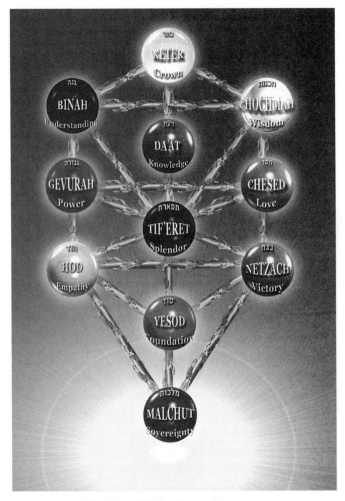

11. The Tree of Life: Linear Representation

reflects the implicit or explicit judgmentalism of the person who suffers from *Binah* dysfunction. Therefore, if the dysfunctional behavior is emotional blockage and interpersonal distance, the spiritual *tikkun* is the search for and practice of those *mitzvot* (meritorious acts) that open us to other people's needs and encourage a response to those needs.

Rabbi Cordovero puts it this way in *The Palm Tree of Deborah:*

> It is the nature of Wisdom to provide for all that exists . . . So, too, it is necessary that a man have his eyes open to help the children of Israel in their way, and [that] his thoughts be directed to bringing near those who have strayed and [nonjudgmentally] to *think well of them* [emphasis added] . . . Furthermore, Wisdom preserves the life of all things . . . So he, too, should teach life to the whole populace of the world and cause them to possess the life of this world and the next and provide them with a means of living. To sum up, he should cause life to flow for all . . . And he should constantly pray for mercy and blessing for the world just as the Supernal Father has mercy on all His creatures. And he should constantly pray for the alleviation of suffering, as if those who suffer were actually his [own] children and as if he had created them . . . Furthermore, his mercy should extend to all creatures, neither destroying nor despising any of them. For the Supernal Wisdom is extended to all created things— minerals, plants, animals and humans . . . This is the reason our Holy Teacher [Rabbi Judah the Prince] was punished for his failure to have pity on the young calf which tried to hide near him [from the slaughterer], saying to him: "Go, for this thou wast created." Therefore, sufferings, which are derived from the aspect of Judgment, came upon him, for mercy acts as a shield before Judgment. And when he [Rabbi Judah] took pity on a weasel [which his servant was about to harm], saying: "It is written: 'And His tender mercies are over all His works,' " he was delivered from Judgment because he drew upon him-

self the light of Wisdom, and the sufferings were taken
away. (pp. 81–83)

We can put this into practice by paying careful attention to signs
that our loved ones are hurting. We should avoid rationalizing their
pain away and blaming and shaming them for their suffering.
Instead, we should validate their feelings, and attempt to relate
them to our own remembered experiences of pain. Furthermore,
we should take the time to visit people who are ill, comfort the
bereaved, and offer financial support to those who need our help.

Rabbi Cordovero's comment about caring for animals should
not be taken lightly. Our pets are totally dependent upon us, and
their love is unconditional. We should repay their love with tender
care. It goes without saying that we should avoid cruelty to animals, remembering that permission to eat animal flesh was grudg-
ingly granted by God "because the inclination of man is evil from
his youth" (Gen. 8:21). This is why the Torah surrounds the eating
of meat with many ritual prohibitions.

TIKKUN OF DA'AT

Our case studies have shown that such dysfunctions of *Da'at* as
commitment phobias, procrastination, indecision, and impetuous
decision making stem from our inability to forgive ourselves for
real and (mostly) imaginary poor decisions, mistakes, and failings.
For this reason, the therapeutic strategies I suggest emphasize training in self-forgiveness. This recommendation is based not only on
sound, accepted psychological principles, but also on the spiritual
teachings of Rabbi Cordovero. Strictly speaking, his *tikkun* relates
to the perfection of *Binah.* However, since *Da'at* synthesizes the
activities of *Chochmah* and *Binah,* his *Binah* correction can also be
applied to *Da'at.* Again, I quote from *The Palm Tree of Deborah.*

How shall a man train himself to acquire the quality of Understanding [or, as we have explained, *Da'at*]? It is to be acquired by returning in perfect repentance, than which nothing is more important, for it rectifies every flaw. Just as it is the function of Understanding to sweeten all judgments and to neutralize their bitterness, so man should repent and rectify every flaw . . . and the days of his life will be crowned according to the secret of the Supernal Repentance . . . For you must not say that repentance is good only for the holy portion in man but also for the portion of evil which is sweetened after the fashion of this quality . . . Do not think that there is no hope for you because you belong to the evil side. This is false . . . Man turns his evil deeds themselves into good so that his intentional sins become good deeds . . . Therefore, man purifies the evil inclination and brings it into the good so that it becomes rooted above in the holy. This is the high degree of repentance, which he who follows should ponder on each day and repeat in some measure each day. (pp. 86–88)

True repentance requires us to forgive ourselves and others, even as we ask for God's forgiveness. Our forgiveness of ourselves and others brings healing from the guilt and self-blame that cripples us. Just as God's forgiveness helps us to achieve at-one-ment with him, our forgiveness of ourselves and others helps us achieve at-one-ment with ourselves.

12

REBALANCING OUR *SEFIROT*
OF FEELING

—◆◈◆—

Although human beings are blessed with reason, our lives and relationships are more commonly influenced by our hearts than our heads. Our emotions are mediated by the *Ru'ach* dimension of our soul and by *Chesed, Gevurah,* and *Tif'eret.* The *Ru'ach* is like the central exchange mechanism of a complex interlocking system. It can both influence and be influenced by the other two parts of the incarnated soul—the *Nefesh,* its "animal" dimension, and the *Neshamah,* its cognitive dimension. It follows that when our *Sefirot* of feeling are out of balance and distorted by the *kelipot* of the *sitra achra,* all our faculties—our ability to think rationally and relate meaningfully—are severely compromised. Furthermore, all human activities have cosmic consequences. Therefore, the bad news is that distortions in our *Sefirot* of feeling impede the repair of the world. But there is also good news. Repairing our *Sefirot* of feeling brings healing to ourselves and the world.

REPAIRING THE *SEFIRAH* OF *CHESED*

The damage inflicted by the *kelipot* is usually systemic, and causes our *sefirah* triads to be thrown off balance. Each story I have shared with you has illustrated a single *sefirah* dysfunction. I use the case studies as a simple way of describing specific *sefirah* imbalances and useful interventions. In reality, however, none of the stories I have shared was as simple as I have made out. In every instance, there were multiple *sefirah* imbalances.

By now, you will probably be able to diagnose imbalances in different parts of your own *sefirah* system. The trick is to use all the applicable interventions that are suggested in the individual case studies. From my own story, you will have learned about interventions for dysfunctions in *Binah* and *Chochmah*. Unfortunately, there was further damage. My *Chesed* was also severely compromised. So my personal experience can also show people with *Chesed* dysfunction how to move forward.

MY PERSONAL STORY *(continued)*

I have already described my overachievement and workaholism, which were an attempt to compensate for the insecurities triggered by my father's disappearance. This caused imbalance in my *Sefirot* of thinking. My overachievement was in the intellectual realm. The result was my neglect of my *Chochmah* and my intuitive potential. But I also used my analytical way of dealing with problems to maintain emotional distance and keep myself from being hurt again. My *Chesed* was also seriously compromised in another respect. My need for acceptance turned me into a knee-jerk "pleaser." I became a caricature of the *Chesed* personality. I was at everyone's beck and call and was unable to establish firm boundaries. My mantra was "give, give, give." Perhaps this was why I succeeded so well in my rabbinic pastoral work. People felt free to phone me and even to come knocking on my door in the small hours of the morning. The cost to my family was enormous, because I appeared to have time for everyone but them. In retrospect, I understand my muddled thinking. I felt secure in the love of my family and insecure about the love of everybody else. Years later, my children told me how hard it had been for them.

Repairing My Personal Sefirah of Chesed

In addition to reparenting the inner child, the empty chair, and self-esteem training, with which you are now familiar, my therapy program involved the following interventions.

⦿ *Assertiveness Training.* This is the perfect intervention for people who feel guilty whenever they say no. Some of us are uncomfortable about returning something to the store that is not exactly right for us. Neither do we feel good about refusing our friends' unreasonable requests. Does this sound familiar? "I'm going on a trip. Will you please take me to the airport during rush hour tomorrow evening?" What you really want to say is "Can't you take a taxi?" But you are afraid your friend will say, "I would have done it for you." So you put your own needs aside and say, "Of course. What time shall I pick you up?" I was helped a great deal by a book published decades ago and reprinted many times. It is called *When I Say No, I Feel Guilty,* by Manuel Smith. I'd like to quote his reaction to the request for a ride to the airport.

> When I say "no," I feel guilty. But if I say "yes," I will hate myself. When you say this to yourself, your real desires are in conflict with your childhood training, and you find yourself without cues that would prompt you in coping with this conflict. What can you say? If I say "no" will my friend feel hurt and rejected? Will he not like me anymore? Will he think that I'm self-centered, or at least, not very nice? If I don't do it, am I an uncaring so-and-so? If I say "yes"—how come I'm always doing these things? Am I a patsy? Or is this the price I have to pay to live with other people? (p. 24)

Dr. Smith has very effective strategies for self-assertiveness training. I also recommend the chapter on assertiveness training in *Behavior Therapy,* edited by Masters, Burish, Hollon, and Rimm.

◉ *Spiritual Interventions.* I shall get to these interventions after sharing two other stories with you.

OTHER COMMON DYSFUNCTIONS OF
THE *SEFIRAH* OF *CHESED*

There are several other self-defeating behaviors that are characterized by problems in this *Sefirah.* Two are worth discussing because they are so widespread—unwise and harmful relationships, and naive, trusting behavior. I shall tell Jerry's and Greta's stories very briefly, without going into early experiences of loss and disappointment, and without elaborating on their failed strategies for transforming their struggle for survival into the formulas for success that had brought them unhappiness. You will see that although their stories are very different, Jerry and Greta shared a common dysfunctional *sefirah* dynamic. You may also see aspects of your own life mirrored in their stories.

JERRY'S STORY

Jerry came to me in panic because his wife, Sandy, had caught him in bed with another woman and left him. She wanted a divorce. Jerry and Sandy were a high-profile couple. To the outside world, their marriage had seemed perfect, but they had not enjoyed marital intimacy, and their lovemaking was mechanical and unfulfilling. Jerry had begun to seek physical release in uncharacteristic ways. He frequented porno movie houses in distant neighborhoods and engaged in a number of one-night stands, sometimes with prostitutes. His sexual adventures became increasingly risky, and he made little effort to cover his tracks.

The Meaning of Jerry's Story

Jerry suffered from grossly distorted *Chesed/Gevurah* balance. He felt spiritually empty, but that did not prevent him from constantly judging himself. The judgmental attribute of his *Gevurah* was always in high gear. His *Gevurah* had been transformed by the *sitra achra* of his sexuality, cutting him off from both Sandy and himself. Like his *Gevurah,* his *Chesed* had also been transformed by the shadow side of his personality, the *kelipot* of the *Nefesh.* He was unable to receive or give authentic love. Illicit sexual release became a substitute for the intimate relationship for which he yearned.

Interventions

Jerry's therapy program began with self-esteem training and his completion, and continued with the following interventions.

- ◉ *Hypnotherapy.* Jerry was a good subject for hypnosis. My strategy was to create a split screen in his mind. One screen would show him a replay of one of his lurid sexual adventures. The other would present an empowering version of himself talking to an imagined loving companion. The lurid screen would be associated with aversive suggestions. The optimistic screen suggested the possibility of a genuine intimate connection. Jerry learned to hypnotize himself rapidly whenever he experienced the urge for sexual release, and then to switch between the lurid and optimistic screens. It did not take long to extinguish his unhealthy feelings.
- ◉ *Spiritual Work.* The core of Jerry's problem was that he had never tapped into his spiritual potential. His family of origin had been pragmatic and scornful of "all that superstitious religious drivel." He had lived in an existential abyss. He agreed to sign up for a weekly meditation class and also a weekly Torah class. His teacher was astonished by his intuitive spiritual creativity and encouraged him to put his

novel interpretations of Scripture on paper. He discovered that he wrote well and easily, and he considered doing a book about his personal journey for fellow "returnees to Judaism."

◉ *Couples Therapy.* Although the outcome of Jerry and Sandy's couples therapy was divorce, it was healing for both of them. Their divorce was nonconfrontational, and they were able to share their parenting responsibilities in an amicable fashion.

◉ *Social Change.* I supported Jerry in his decision to accept a new job opportunity and move to the East Coast, thus enabling him to build a new life in a different environment.

GRETA'S STORY

Greta was in her late twenties and had been referred to me by her physician following a failed attempt at suicide. When she was a very young girl, her mother had become gravely ill. Unable to cope with both child-rearing and his ailing wife, her father had sent Greta and her brother to his sister. While Greta was with her aunt, her mother passed away, and her father decided that the funeral and burial would be too traumatic for the children. Therefore, Greta had never had an opportunity to say good-bye to her mother and express her grief. She and her brother spent most of their childhood and adolescence with their aunt, since their father was simply unable to take care of them properly.

Greta had become seriously involved with a young man, leaning upon him for emotional support, but he had not treated her well. Notwithstanding the advice of her friends to break off the relationship, she had hung on desperately, accepting his neglect and doing everything in her power to please him. Setting out to please had been her strategy for success throughout her life. It had been her way of ensuring her security in her aunt's home and of making her feel safe at work. Generous to the extreme, she was loved and admired by everybody—except her boyfriend. When he suddenly ended the relationship, she overdosed on sleeping pills.

The Meaning of Greta's Story

Greta's strategy had radically distorted her *Chesed.* Her tolerance of her boyfriend's abusive behavior was irrational. She was never able to give him the ultimatum that her friends had suggested, for fear of hurting his feelings and losing him. Her inappropriate generosity reflected *Chesed* imbalance. She was easily and frequently conned by people who came to her with hard luck stories, because she wanted to please everybody—except herself.

Interventions

Self-esteem therapy, assertiveness training, and role-play prepared Greta not only for her completion, but also for saying no to unreasonable requests and unacceptable behaviors.

- *Completion.* For the first time in her life, Greta was able to summon the courage to speak to her father about the pain she had suffered by being sent away to her aunt's home and denied the opportunity of saying good-bye to her mother. She was also able to accept responsibility for her failed strategies for survival.
- *Inner Child Work.* Greta was able to use this technique to nurture the lonely child she had been.
- *Completion of Grieving.* We worked through the stages of bereavement together, as if the loss had just occurred. Elisabeth Kübler-Ross's five-step strategy for dealing with death in *On Death and Dying* was adapted to help Greta mourn her mother's passing in a healthy way.

Denial. To ease her pain, Greta had denied how much she continued to miss her mother. She had also denied how much her mother must have missed taking care of her and watching her grow up. She addressed her mother in the empty chair and wrote a long letter to her, sharing with her all the painful feelings she had repressed and pouring out her love. Reading the letter at her mother's graveside was cathartic. Guided meditation helped her visualize ongoing scenes of her mother's love for her and continuing participation in her life.

Anger. Greta had never permitted herself to express anger at the cruel hand life had dealt her. Instead, she would often flare into bouts of temper over minor frustrations. Therapy helped her to own her anger. The guided meditations gradually extinguished these emotions, and replaced them with healing, empowering, loving feelings.

Bargaining. People who face death often try to strike a bargain with God: "If you heal me [or so-and-so], I promise that . . ." In the secrecy of her own mind, Greta had made a bargain with her boyfriend: "If I am always kind and loving, you will never leave me." Therapy helped her realize how self-defeating her bargain had been.

Depression. Greta also began to mourn all her lost opportunities and dreams. For example, as she faced the finality of her relationship with her boyfriend, she became increasingly depressed. Martin Seligman's *Learned Optimism: How to Change Your Mind and Your Life,* which deals with the psychology of optimism, provided her with useful tools. She gradually recognized that depression is learned helplessness, and that it can be overcome with learned optimism. Aaron Beck's cognitive restructuring approach to depression was also very helpful to her.

Acceptance. The final stage of Greta's bereavement therapy was accepting the impossibility of renewing her relationship with her boyfriend and planning for a hopeful future without him.

SPIRITUAL INTERVENTIONS

The *tikkun* for inappropriate *Chesed* is the practice of appropriate *Chesed.* Surely, doing things that make you feel good if you say yes beats doing things only because you feel guilty if you say no.

In *The Palm Tree of Deborah,* Rabbi Moses Cordovero begins the chapter on the *tikkun* of *Chesed* with a call for loving service of God. His assumption is that our innate sense of loving-kindness is a gift of grace. We reciprocate God's grace by doing things that enhance our love for him, either by serving him directly, or through our acts of kindness to his creatures. We serve God directly by performing the positive *mitzvot* that heighten our awareness of our relationship with and dependence on him, and by avoiding activities that deflect our consciousness from him. According to Maimonides, our love for God is enhanced as we learn more about the wonders of his Creation, and through our study of his Scriptures. In terms of regular practice, prayer and meditation are the most powerful means of expressing our love for, dependence on, and gratitude to God. The habit of daily prayer enhances this connection. I shall discuss this practice much more fully toward the end of this book.

Although Rabbi Cordovero does not refer to it explicitly in this chapter, meditation is also strongly recommended. Because *Chesed* is directly connected to *Chochmah* on the right side of the Tree of Life, the grace of Divine Wisdom flows from the mind to the heart. The meditation technique for opening *Chochmah* that I outlined in chapter 11 will, therefore, also open blocked *Chesed,* and restore balance in dysfunctional *sefirah* triads of feeling. At the end of this chapter, I shall suggest an additional meditation for rebalancing our *Sefirot* of feeling. Don't limit yourself to the meditations in this book. Any appropriate meditation method will bring healing to your *Chesed.* The important thing is to set regular times for daily meditation. What works best for me is the early morning, before I begin my formal daily worship. This is an age-old Jewish practice. The Talmud relates that pious individuals of former generations would spend an hour before their morning worship in meditation (*B.T. Berachot* 30b). This discipline does more than merely promote personal growth and healing. It also transforms the ritual of daily worship into a self-transcending conversation with God.

The greater part of Rabbi Cordovero's chapter on the development of *Chesed* is based on the virtues prescribed by the sages and included as an introductory passage to the Jewish morning service. The practice of charity is of particular importance in this context. Many people with *Chesed* problems are reluctant to part with their money. The fund-raiser's pitch "give till it hurts" does not apply to them. For them, giving always hurts. In contrast, many people have the opposite problem. They feel guilty whenever they say no. Their philanthropy is indiscriminate and profligate. Jewish law helps modify these problems by setting lower and upper limits (no less than 10 percent and no more than 20 percent of after-tax income). It also sets standards for prioritizing our giving. In this way, we accustom ourselves to giving charity both responsibly and without guilt. Rabbi Cordovero's elaboration of the cosmic effects of virtuous practice differentiates his treatment from the more commonplace rabbinic commentaries. For example, he recommends that we find opportunities to visit the sick, because according to the Kabbalah, the *Shekhinah* attaches itself to those who are ill. Therefore, our active concern for them elevates the *Shekhinah* as well, raising *Malchut* in all the hidden and revealed universes.

The standard catalog of virtues includes participating in the last rites for the deceased. Rabbi Cordovero describes the spiritual effects of this act of nonreciprocal kindness. The ritual of cleansing the deceased and clothing them in white shrouds is "the cleansing of the *Sefirot* in the white hot fire provided by the light of the good deed, to elevate them, according to the secret of the unity, to bind them above" (p. 99). Also, the effect of hospitality is to invite the bounty of *Tif'eret* and *Yesod* into our realm, *Malchut*. Rabbi Cordovero treats the virtues of charity, bringing the bride to the marriage canopy, and making peace between man and his neighbor in the same way. His chapter on *Chesed* is well worth reading.

REPAIRING THE *SEFIRAH* OF *GEVURAH*

Do you remember Yasmin's story? Her tale is a vivid example of *Gevurah* imbalance. It reflects the most common characteristics of the effects of a dysfunctional *Gevurah*.

YASMIN'S STORY *(continued)*

In chapter 6, you were introduced to Yasmin, the overachieving, self-doubting child of a brutal Moroccan father. You may recall that Yasmin became a professor of international relations at a prestigious university. However, in spite of her success, she was desperately unhappy. She was not only overly judgmental of others, but also of herself. Beneath her veneer of accomplishment and competence, she was frightened and insecure. She was willing to give up on opportunities for professional advancement for fear of having to confront powerful colleagues. After all, they might not like her and might under-mine her if she challenged them.

Yasmin was certain that people who were at least as bright as her father would eventually discover that she was really not as competent as she had made out. Because of her self-doubts, she was also excessively guarded in her relationships, convinced that any male friend she allowed to penetrate her defenses would reject her as a fraud. She called herself a "male repeller."

The Meaning of Yasmin's Story

Yasmin had learned from her early childhood experiences that the world was not safe, and her strategy was to become inde-pendent, competitive, and successful. This may have helped to protect her from her father's brutality, but it had become a problem instead of a solution. Her primitive defenses were the *kelipot* that eventually enveloped her in a coat of constricting armor, but the shell with which she had surrounded herself had not concealed her self-doubt. It had only served to mask her true personality and to throw her *Binah, Gevurah,* and *Chesed* out of balance. She played mind games to distance her from her feelings (*Binah* distortion), was overly defended (*Gevurah* distortion), and became an inveterate pleaser, inca-pable of giving real love (*Chesed* distortion).

Interventions

It took a number of sessions before Yasmin was ready to trust me enough to open up. Yasmin was so enveloped by her *kelipot* defenses that she had no sense of who she really was. She confided that she had long ago lost touch with her femininity and that her model for survival was masculine. When I asked her to describe the self that was hiding beneath her armor, she said, "I see myself as a formless glob seeping out under my shell." In addition to emotional journaling, self-forgiveness, assertiveness training, and role-play, with which you are familiar, Yasmin found the following very helpful.

- ◉ *Completion.* Yasmin's biggest problem was accepting responsibility for how she had scripted her life. Therefore, the completion exercise was very difficult for her. She had severed all contact with her family many years before and did not wish to reestablish communication with them. We needed to work out a method of achieving completion with her parents that would keep her safe and also enable her to take full responsibility for her failed strategies. We finally agreed that she would write a detailed letter to each of her parents, expressing her anger and pain about their contribution to her unhappy childhood. She would make it very clear that they had caused her enormous pain, but that they were not responsible for the way she had subsequently fashioned her life. Yasmin was very tearful when she read the letters aloud in my office, but as wrenching as the exercise had been, it was cathartic, and she was now ready to take control of her life.
- ◉ *Relaxation.* Yasmin was always tense and usually kept her legs crossed and her arms folded over her chest. We began relaxation training with breathing exercises: deep diaphragm inhalation and blowing out tension with every exhalation. We proceeded to muscle relaxation. Yasmin tensed and released her muscles, moving from her feet to her calves and thighs, and becoming aware of her weight on the couch. She repeated the process with her arms, shoulders, neck, mouth, cheeks, and eyes and allowed her diaphragm breathing to lower her pulse rate. She contracted to practice this twice daily for a week.
- ◉ *Guided Meditation.* We proceeded to a variation of the guided meditation at the end of this chapter. The starting

point was her recognition of the lovableness of the "glob" beneath her *kelipot*. We used the "hidden light" in her glob as the starting point for the meditation.

⊙ *Intuition Awareness and Dream Journaling.* Yasmin undertook to keep a journal of her dreams and intuitions, even though she had previously been dismissive of both. Now she allowed herself to ask what her "inner self" was trying to tell her. She also wrote down ways in which she was guided by her intuition in her everyday activities.

⊙ *Reclaiming the Feminine.* Yasmin acknowledged that it was time she did things to make her feel good as a woman instead of just being successful as an academic. She would set aside time for massages and facials, and pay a weekly visit to a hairdresser and manicurist. She would modify her wardrobe, finally saying a decisive no to her deceased father's comments about the futility of her ever finding a really pretty dress.

⊙ *Social Empowerment.* Yasmin resolved to try to enjoy future dates without looking for flaws in the men she dated. Should she be unable to overlook a flaw, she would explore in therapy whether she was using her old defenses, or whether the flaw was real and, if so, how she might communicate her concerns to her date without necessarily sabotaging a potential relationship. She began to calculate the emotional cost of possible disappointment against the benefit of finding a friend and partner for life.

SPIRITUAL INTERVENTIONS

The Kabbalah presumes an intrinsic connection between the *sitra achra* and the exercise of power and independence. As you have seen, the original shattering of the vessels was the result of the non-connectedness of the *Sefirot* prior to their reconstitution in the Tree of Life as we now know it. Because like attracts like, when radically independent people are unwilling or unable to connect with others, they attract fragments of the shattered vessels, the *kelipot* of the *sitra achra,* thus distorting their *Gevurah.*

In rabbinic literature, the *sitra achra* is identified with the inclination to evil **(yetzer ha-ra),** which motivates our will to dominate and judge others harshly. The rabbis also identify the *yetzer ha-ra* with the sex drive. When this *Nefesh* energy is unrestrained, it leads to illicit and, sometimes, abusive relationships, but when it is controlled and transformed into holy energy, it leads to healthy sexual activity. "Were it not for the *yetzer ha-ra,* people would not build homes, marry, have families, and civilize their surroundings" (*Midrash Rabbah,* Gen. 9:7). Rabbi Moses Cordovero's strategy in *The Palm Tree of Deborah* for repairing *Gevurah* is a kabbalistic application of this rabbinic passage.

> For his wife's sake, he should gently bestir his evil inclination in the direction of the sweet Powers, to provide her with clothes and with a house, for example, and he should say: "By providing her with clothes, I adorn the *Shekhinah,* for the *Shekhinah* is adorned with Understanding which is [also] Power (for it includes all Powers, and these are sweetened in Her abundant mercies). Therefore, all the needs of the household are **tikkunim** of the *Shekhinah,* which is sweetened by means of the evil inclination, which was created to do the will of his Creator and for no other purpose." (p. 103)

In this passage, Rabbi Cordovero is emphasizing that recoil from giving and receiving love is the effect of a dysfunctional *Gevurah.* Its antidote is to give more love. When *Chesed* is awakened, the manipulative I-it relationship is transformed into an I-thou relationship. I shall return to this theme when I discuss the repair of *Yesod*.

REPAIRING THE *SEFIRAH* OF *TIF'ERET*

The ancient Greeks defined beauty as truth and harmony, which is reminiscent of the Kabbalah's understanding of the function of *Tif'eret* as the synthesis of *Chesed* and *Gevurah*. Therefore, the symptoms of a dysfunctional *Tif'eret* include dishonesty and hypocrisy. Leonard's tale, which I began to relate in chapter 6, explains one of the possible origins of this dysfunction and how it relates to the more general imbalance of the *Sefirot* of feeling. Unfortunately, *Tif'eret* dysfunction is all too common, so many of you will think I am talking not only about Leonard's experience but also about a problem you have had.

LEONARD'S STORY *(continued)*

You may recall that Leonard's strategy for avoiding trouble was to lie about culpable behaviors and that much of his life had become a lie—his business practices, his marriage, and his philanthropic posturing. His deceitful gestures of concern for the needy and the mind games he played with his wife were clear evidence of *Chesed* distortion and *Gevurah* imbalance, while his dishonesty showed the extent to which his *Tif'eret* had transformed into its own shadow. Although Leonard had learned to get away with it, he saw himself as an inauthentic person, a cheat, and hypocrite, always on the verge of exposure.

Interventions

As with all my clients, I suggested two types of intervention for Leonard, kabbalistic/spiritual and psychotherapeutic, which were undertaken in tandem.

The formal clinical interventions included self-esteem, self-assertiveness, self-forgiveness, systematic desensitization, role-play in preparation for completion, and completion. In addition, the following interventions proved to be effective.

- *Dishonesty Journal.* In an adaptation of emotional journaling, Leonard contracted to keep a journal of his distortions of truth. This involved a review of each day before he went to bed—focusing on every interaction he had had with others on the phone, in writing, in e-mails, or in person. His journal would have four headings: *Event, Distortion, Feelings About the Distortion,* and *Alternative Appropriate Response.*
- *Couples Therapy.* Leonard was aware of the risks of couples therapy, but hoped that his commitment to honesty would help his wife forgive his past behavior. As is so often the case, his wife had been aware of his duplicity for a long time, but had been too frightened to deal with the issues directly. Their couple's work together was a blessing to them both.
- *Cognitive Social Involvement.* Leonard had a good background in Torah studies, because he'd attended a yeshiva through high school. He now undertook to tutor a student who was learning disabled and lived with his widowed mother. This was an effective therapy for his atrophied *Chesed,* and helped restore his *Chesed/Gevurah* balance. Gradually, he became the boy's Big Brother, and came to love him in spite of his problems. Their association taught him that giving and receiving love is not conditional upon perfection. In therapy, Leonard learned to translate this experience into his own life situation, and acknowledge that people would love him just for being who he really was. It is difficult to know who gained more

from this intervention: Leonard, his student, or his family and associates.

Let me say a word about the spiritual interventions for *Tif'eret* rebalancing. *Tif'eret* is the medium for the Torah of Truth. Therefore, its enhancement centers around the teaching of Torah. Rabbi Cordovero emphasizes that the teaching of Torah presents challenges to *Gevurah* and opportunities to *Chesed.* A teacher can relate to a student from a place of power, fear, and control, or with love and sensitivity. The effect of using love and sensitivity is to bring Beauty into the realm of *Malchut.* Sovereignty and power are thus "sweetened" throughout the cosmos. Leonard undertook to meditate regularly. While many meditation modalities are effective, the special meditation for rebalancing the *Sefirot* of feeling at the end of this chapter was particularly helpful for Leonard and will benefit people with similar problems.

⊙ *Meditation for Rebalancing the* Sefirot *of Feeling.* This meditation is described in detail below. Leonard committed himself to fifteen minutes of daily meditation.

MEDITATION FOR
REBALANCING THE SEFIROT OF FEELING

The following meditation is adapted from the teachings of my friend and colleague Professor Kenneth N. Klee, and his great teachers.

1. Bring yourself into a state of preparedness and relaxation as described on pages 44–46, numbers 1–17.
2. Breathe slowly and rhythmically through your nose. Do not hold your breath during the meditation.
3. Put your awareness in your heart, the seat of your *Ru'ach.*
4. Think about someone you love, expanding that love to love for God and all his creatures.

5. Picture the love in your heart as a glowing ember. Watch its light become brighter, filling your heart and permeating your entire chest.

6. Be aware of your inborn potential for love, kindness, tenderness, and compassion.

7. Take a breath and exhale, moving the love in your heart from *Chesed* to the center of your crown.

8. Be aware of the flow of light between your heart and head, between your *Chesed* and *Chochmah*.

9. Validate the love in your heart and the light in your mind by silently giving thanks for this love and awareness.

10. Say the following prayer to yourself: "O, *Havayah,* make me an instrument of your peace and tranquillity."

11. Feel the inner peace within you, allowing yourself to be a clear and perfect channel for divine peace.

12. Let the peace flow from your heart to your arms and hands.

13. Imagine the earth as a small ball before you. Send vibrations of peace to it and bless the earth with peace.

14. Feel divine love within you. Allow yourself to be a clear and perfect channel of divine love.

15. Be aware of all fear and hatred leaving you, floating away gently, like wisps of cloud.

16. Let the love flow from your heart, through your arms to your hands, and bless the earth with peace and love.

17. Feel the spirit of reconciliation within you.

18. Allow yourself to be a clear and perfect channel for divine forgiveness and reconciliation.

19. Watch all your grudges leave you, floating away like wisps of cloud.

20. Let reconciliation flow from your heart through your arms to your hands.

21. Bless the earth with the spirit of forgiveness, reconciliation, understanding, harmony, and peace.

22. Experience divine loving-kindness as a light that fills your heart and spreads throughout your body.

23. Watch the all-encompassing light of divine love move

down from above your head toward you, enveloping and caressing you.

24. Allow yourself to be a clear and perfect channel of divine love and kindness.

25. Feel the inner light of your love and the surrounding aura of God's love merge, making you a body of light and love.

26. Let your love flow through your arms and hands, blessing the earth with love.

27. Allow yourself to bask in your own light, love, harmony, peace, and forgiveness for a few minutes.

28. When you are ready, gently open your eyes.

29. Journal what you felt and experienced during this meditation.

13

REBALANCING OUR *SEFIROT* OF RELATING

———◆———

In chapter 6, you were introduced to ideal human relationships. I drew your attention to the enormous difference between loving in general and focusing one's love upon one particular person. Love in general requires no commitment. By definition, it is ephemeral, moving from person to person. Indeed, the highest form of *Chesed* is an anonymous act of kindness, requiring no ongoing connection between giver and receiver. To all intents and purposes, each is merely an object to the other, and their relationship is I-it rather than I-thou.

In contrast, *Netzach* governs the relationship between two persons. *Hod* further defines it as being between two people who value and respect the otherness of the other person. It does not permit him or her to be swallowed up or effaced by his or her partner, and neither person can be reduced to an object. An "I" who relates authentically to a "thou" cannot exploit the other.

The idyllic dance of the I and thou requires each to give to the other and allow the other to retain his or her uniqueness. Unfortunately, in real life, the dance is often anything but idyllic, and many people manipulate those who look to them for love, often treating them like doormats. Such dysfunctional relationships reflect the imbalance of *Netzach, Hod,* and *Yesod.* When we heal and rebalance these damaged *Sefirot,* we replace manipulation with reciprocity, transforming I-it relationships into satisfying I-thou commitments.

REPAIRING THE *SEFIRAH* OF *NETZACH*

Dysfunction of one *Sefirah* is almost always associated with the dysfunction of other *Sefirot,* but in the next example, since the primary dysfunction is associated with the *Netzach,* the development of its dark side is given special attention.

MAX'S STORY

Max came to see me because his marriage was breaking up. Ilana, his wife, had long suggested that they go for marital counseling, but Max had refused, saying, "Only crazies and emotional cretins need professionals to help them sort out their problems." Eventually, Ilana sought therapy on her own, and her therapist supported her decision to leave her husband. Max was not coming to see me for therapy but, as he put it, because "you are a rabbi. You believe in marriage. She respects you. Maybe you can talk her out of her nonsense and get her to come back to me with the kids." I gently informed Max that the problem was probably much deeper than he realized, and I would need to see him and Ilana, separately and together, in order to help them. I would not agree to "sort her out" and "put some sense into her head." Max reluctantly agreed to talk to me on my terms.

Max was the son of middle-class, suburban parents. His father worked hard and adored his wife, Max's mother, even though she was extremely self-absorbed. Max's earliest memories of disappointment involved his mother's withdrawal of her love to "bring him into line." He recalled displeasing her on several occasions. Sometimes, he had simply been disobedient.

At others, he had tried to please her but was unable to give her the kind of ego gratification she needed. He had been hurt and bewildered when she responded, "I can't love a little boy who doesn't make me happy."

As Max grew older, he noticed that his mother manipulated his father in the same way. When he would not submit to her unreasonable demands, he was subjected to the silent treatment until he apologized abjectly, gave her gifts, and promised to do exactly what she wanted. It did not take Max too long to learn his mother's game. Its rules were simple: You get people to love you, and when they care for you, you can threaten to withdraw your love. Then you can get almost anything you want out of them, because they are scared to lose your love. Max followed in his mother's footsteps. He was good-looking and charismatic. Girls would do almost anything to win his affection. But whenever he became bored or simply juiced up by the challenge of a new conquest, he would discard his current girlfriend. Yet despite his bevy of girls, he was depressed. He reckoned that he must be unhappy because he was single. Most of his friends were married and had kids and seemed to be happy. So Max decided to get married. But marriage did not alter what he had learned about the world as a child, nor did it change his attitude. It merely exchanged a series of temporary relationships for a permanent one, with some secret liaisons on the side for excitement. This worked until Ilana announced that she was leaving him.

The Meaning of Max's Story

In terms of accepted psychological theory, Max's problem was not difficult to diagnose. He was narcissistic—plain and simple. Kabbalistic psychology, however, permitted me a deeper understanding. Max's life script had required him to gratify his impulses. This unabashed hedonism reflected the encrustation of his *Nefesh*. Its role had transformed from survival needs to the drive for endless gratification. Nothing physical was off limits, provided his needs were satisfied. His *Ru'ach* had also fallen prey to the *sitra achra*. Early in his childhood, it had given up on motivating him to refine his instincts. Instead, it became more and more inflamed by them. His *Neshamah* was also encrusted, and he could no longer use reason to guide his feelings and actions. Instead, his *Neshamah* rationalized his self-centered behavior. No wonder Max had not understood Ilana's pain. Like everybody else in his life, she had become an object for the fulfillment of his desires.

This process all but extinguished Max's inner light, making him an empty vessel. When pushed, he could not say who he really was—apart from the way he had become defined by his failed strategies. His life was devoid of responsibility and existential meaning. His girlfriends, his wife, and his children notwithstanding, Max was painfully lonely. He was depressed because he was spiritually empty. He personified the dark side of *Netzach*. He was totally manipulative, and his relationships never rose beyond the I-it level, but his soul longed for authentic connection.

Interventions

Because Max's problem was primarily spiritual, he could not become whole without finding meaning in his life. Therefore, after a few exploratory sessions, I suggested to Max that we try both spiritual and psychological approaches to healing. I also suggested that he tell Ilana that he was in therapy, and share with her what he had so far discovered about himself, letting her know that whatever happened between them, he was committed to dealing with his own problems. He also offered to join her in couples therapy with a counselor of her choice when he was further along the path of psychospiritual healing—if she were still open to making their marriage work.

In preparation for completion, Max did inner child work and role-playing.

- ◉ *Completion.* Max had never accepted responsibility, believing he had become what he was because of his mother's example, and resenting her for his unhappiness. Unless Max could accept full responsibility for his life, his meeting with his parents would be inauthentic. After a few sessions, Max was able to see that he alone had authored his self-defeating life script and arranged to meet with his parents. His mother was immediately defensive, and responded to his description of his losses in a passive-aggressive manner. However, Max insisted on having his full say. Although he was not convinced that his mother understood the purpose of the encounter, it did not really matter. It was enough for him to have accepted responsibility for his own life in the presence of the woman he had come to blame for everything that had gone wrong.

- ◉ *Forgiveness.* Max was aware of how he had used other people and was ready to ask for their forgiveness. It was far more difficult for him to learn to forgive himself. Probing discussions of Maimonides's stages of atonement were very helpful to him in his search for personal at-one-ment. Since his guilt in this respect was real rather than neurotic, his acceptance of responsibility and his resolution to change made self-forgiveness less difficult to achieve.

- ◉ *Social Involvement. Netzach* dysfunction is closely related to *Chesed* dysfunction. Complete self-absorption is a sure sign of an inability to give love and show real kindness to others. Before Max could focus his love on anyone, he had to awaken his dormant *Chesed* channels.

Max agreed to volunteer at a pediatric AIDS clinic on his afternoon off, and to work one evening a week in a homeless shelter. His exposure to the hopelessness and pain of children and their families moved him from self-absorption to other-directedness. He became particularly attached to a ten-year-old girl, since he had a ten-year-old child of his own. To his surprise, he became overwhelmingly saddened by the child's decline, and was devastated when she died. His duties at the shelter also evoked other feelings. Many of the clients were addicts. His own life had been different in many ways, but it was also uncannily similar, and he saw that, like them, he was also paying the price of his hedonism.

Rabbi Moses Cordovero had written of the imperative to learn from all people. Nobody, no matter what their status in life, is without something to teach. It was in this sense that the psalmist declared, "From all my teachers have I gotten understanding" (Ps. 119:99). Ben Zoma, a second-century sage, had interpreted this verse to mean, "Who is wise? He who learns from all men" (*Avot* 4:1). Rabbi Cordovero, therefore, included the development of openness to learn from the experience and wisdom of others among his *tikkunim* for *Netzach*. After all, genuine respect for others is the antithesis of the self-absorption of a *kelipah*-encrusted *Netzach*. What Max gained from his experience at the homeless center was empathy. The heart of the former narcissist was finally opened to the pain and suffering of others, and the more he gave of himself, the less depressed he felt.

◉ *Meditation.* To help Max restore his *Chochmah, Chesed,* and *Netzach* to health, I suggested that he spend twenty minutes a day in guided meditation. In addition to the meditations included in this book, Max used Aryeh Kaplan's volumes on

Jewish meditation and Jeffrey Thompson's theta meditation system to help develop his own meditative style.

⦿ *Couples Therapy.* Ilana opted to join Max for couples therapy. She was happy with the changes she was already seeing in her husband, and considered couples therapy with me as a logical next step for both of them. At my suggestion, she agreed to continue individual therapy with her own therapist. We used the following couples therapy techniques.

Clear Communication. Wade Luquet's *Short-Term Couples Therapy* contains an excellent description of clear communication, based on Harville Hendrix's Imago Model of couples therapy. Chapters 2 and 3 are must-reads. Luquet permits duplication of the exercises appended to the book, and so I was able to give Max and Ilana the exercises covering the work we had done together as homework assignments to be reviewed at the next session. Ilana's therapist had been working with her on self-assertiveness. The safety of my office was an ideal place for her to assert her own needs fearlessly. Max was helped to become an active, empathic listener, showing her that he understood what she was saying, and that he was trying to understand her feelings. She, in turn, let Max know that she understood his genuine remorse about his behaviors.

Couples Journaling. Max and Ilana journaled the kindnesses, special things, and surprises they had given and received. They also noted the rough spots, angry outbursts, hurt or sullen withdrawal and silence, and poor communication. Together, we explored both the good things that had happened during the week and the meaning of the difficult things. We worked on their communication problems using the techniques they were mastering in their homework exercises.

Marital Expectations Contract. They each ranked their expectations from the marriage and from each other in order of importance. This became the basis for more therapeutic exploration. They soon deleted those items that they decided were not critically important and drew up an expectations contract. This contract was task based as well as emotion based. They undertook to record in their couples journals the old and new behaviors of their spouses and the feelings these generated. This helped them to keep track of their progress.

Emotional Openness. Max and Ilana began to share issues that had come up in their individual therapies. Ilana was able to let Max know that she had stayed in the marriage only because of her fear of loss of love, and because she had believed she was not worthy of anything better. Max shared his failed narcissistic success strategies with her. He described the process of completion with his parents, and his acceptance of responsibility. Their sharing brought a new intimacy into their relationship.

Social Involvement. Ilana volunteered to join Max in his work at the pediatric AIDS center and homeless shelter.

Spiritual Awareness. Ilana and Max agreed to become more involved in the life of their religious community, attending services together and committing themselves to participate in a weekly synagogue-based class on religious texts and issues. This would enable a mutual opening of their *Sefirot* of cognition and mindfulness. They decided to gradually introduce the magic and enchantment of religious observance into their home. Ilana and their daughter began to light Sabbath and festival candles, and Max inaugurated the Sabbath and festivals with the blessings over wine. They considered these observances as a tentative first step in their spiritual growth. They spoke

about doing a short daily meditation together. Max himself suggested that he purchase tefillin and wear them
during his meditation time with Ilana. You will learn
about the meaning and significance of tefillin later in the
book (pages 273–275).

⦿ *Family Therapy.* Finally, their children joined them for a few
sessions. Neither Max nor Ilana had any idea how well their
children understood what had been going on. The aim of
the therapy was to allow free expression of anger and fear
and to help all of them to establish new family rules, with
greater participation by the children. The interested reader
will discover a wealth of information on family therapy in
Irene Goldenberg and Herbert Goldenberg's *Family Therapy: An Overview.*

REPAIRING THE *SEFIRAH* OF *HOD*

SUSANNAH'S STORY *(continued)*

In chapter 7, I introduced you to Susannah. Her story is difficult to forget, so you will probably recall that her stepfather
abused her sexually from when she was eight through her
adolescence, that her mother was unable to stop the abuse, and
how the abuse and neglect influenced her subsequent self-
defeating intimate relationships.

I think you should know about Susannah's failed therapies
to better understand how she and I worked on her problems.
Susannah had had many years of therapy, working on her
anger toward her stepfather and, especially, her mother. That,
she thought, was surely the root of her unhappiness. Nothing,
it seemed, could be done about her stepfather, who was senile
and in a nursing home. One therapist had suggested that she
go to see him to express her rage at how he had destroyed her

life. That well-meaning counselor had even offered to join her in the confrontation so that she would feel safer. She had gone to the nursing home and vented her spleen, but the old man had not even recognized her. Needless to say, the encounter gave her no relief. Another therapist had suggested that she put her feelings on paper and burn what she had written, imagining that she was burning the old man and finally removing him from her life. This imaginative strategy, too, had failed. A third had strengthened her for her confrontation with her mother by role-playing the encounter, but the therapist had not foreseen the mother's reaction. The elderly woman simply broke down and wept, telling Susannah how guilty she felt at not having been an adequate protector. This guilt, she said, had crippled her for two decades. Susannah left the meeting feeling even worse than before. Her own pain had been compounded by the knowledge that she had unwittingly contributed to her mother's psychologically depleted state. If only Susannah had been stronger and different, she thought, she might have been able to give her mother the support she had needed. The cognitive therapist she had seen had also seemed to make perfect sense. It was surely Susannah's irrational thinking that had led to her feelings of low self-esteem. When she learned how to reframe her cognitive errors, the feelings that accompanied her thoughts of worthlessness would also go away. Sadly for Susannah, cognitive restructuring had been as unsuccessful as object relations therapy and the other therapies she had tried.

Susannah's Insight

Most of the therapeutic techniques Susannah had tried have been clinically validated. Object relations therapy is very effective in reversing the effects of poor parenting. Cognitive restructuring has been shown to be one of the most effective methods of dealing with depression. Assertiveness training is one of the best ways of raising poor self-esteem. Role-playing is a wonderful technique for preparing for difficult encounters. So why had Susannah failed to gain relief?

You may remember that Susannah had become hysterical and bolted from one of my workshops when it dawned on her that she had not accepted any responsibility for her life. After she had calmed down, she realized that she was finally ready not only to deal with her anger at her mother's weakness, but also to take full responsibility for how she had disempowered herself. She agreed to visit her mother that evening to tell her that although she had been angry for a long time, she was now able to get past that by owning up to her subsequent self-defeating patterns of behavior. She also undertook to write a letter to her stepfather, which she would read to the group and then publicly tear up. During the session the next morning, she took the microphone for the first time, sharing her story and the details of her completion encounter with her mother, and reading and tearing up the letter to her stepfather. The members of the group gave her a standing ovation for her candor and strength. The entire experience was cathartic, but Susannah decided to enroll in a short follow-up series to work out some of her unresolved issues.

Interventions

When first I introduced you to Susannah, I pointed out that her experience was a textbook example of sexual abuse, and that the psychodynamics of her depression were clear. But the damage went deeper, to her very soul. Her strategy for dealing with her wounds had distorted her *Hod.* Had her *Hod* and *Netzach* been in balance, she would have been able to allow space for significant others to be themselves, while at the same time also asserting her own needs. But she had completely denied her needs and personality. She had become psychologically and spiritually invisible and isolated. I suspected that following Susannah's successful completion and acceptance of responsibility, many of the interventions that had failed before might now be effective in conjunction with important additional psychospiritual strategies. Therefore, in addition to inner child work, self-esteem and assertiveness training, and systematic desensitization (mainly to extinguish her fear of confrontation), we used the following interventions.

- ◉ *Guided Meditation and Visualization.* Susannah's spiritual emptiness needed to be filled. I asked her to bring a tape recorder, and we did the Meditation on Being described on pages 44–47 to give her a sense of connectedness. She did this every day for a week, and journaled her experiences. In the second week, we did the Theta Meditation outlined on pages 188–191. I felt it was important for Susannah to learn to trust her intuition. She taped this meditation and promised to do it daily for three weeks, again keeping a record of her experience. After that, we recorded the Meditation for Rebalancing the *Sefirot* of Feeling outlined on pages 214–216 to help her feel good about herself and others. She undertook to do this daily for three weeks, journaling her feelings. I referred her to a number of books with other meditative techniques, encouraging her to find the path that worked best for her. In addition to the works by Aryeh Kaplan that I have already mentioned, I recommended Patrick Fanning's *Visualization for Change* and Marlene Hunter's *Creative Scripts for Hypnotherapy.*
- ◉ *Forgiveness.* Susannah had already forgiven her mother for her weakness and silent collusion in her suffering, but she needed to forgive herself for how she had scripted her life and for having allowed herself to be further abused

as an adult. Combined with meditation, her work on self-forgiveness was more effective than it might have been by itself.

- *Rescripting.* Susannah had already accepted responsibility for the life script she had written. She now agreed that if a bad script could do such harm, a good script could bring healing. She listed her new expectations from life in general, and from men in particular. She also scripted her rules for future relationships. This exercise itself was enormously empowering.
- *Social Involvement.* Susannah's shift from her role as victim required her to assume a positively empowering role. She did this by training to be a volunteer at a shelter for abused women, eventually helping to facilitate group discussions. The deeper object of this intervention was to replace her negative *Hod* energy with positive *Netzach* energy.

REPAIRING THE *SEFIRAH* OF *YESOD*

As you have learned, healthy *Yesod* expresses itself primarily in the loving sexual embrace of husband and wife, whose connection establishes a mutuality of giving and receiving. The lovers become open channels for the focused energies of *Netzach* and the passive energies of *Hod.* Their embrace is transformative, transcending the physical, and opening a window to the Divine. Through their tender love for each other, they experience the tender embrace of God. Maimonides alludes to this experience in his codification of Jewish law, *Mishneh Torah:* **Hilkhot Teshuvah** (*Laws of Repentance* 10:3):*

---

* The *Mishneh Torah* is Maimonides' magisterial code, based on millennia of the oral tradition and drawing on the Babylonian and Jerusalem Talmuds, halakhic *midrash,* and subsequent legal decisions. It is organized in fourteen volumes, each of which is subdivided into different collections of law. The *Laws of Repentance* are part of the first book. The numbers refer to chapter and paragraph.

What is appropriate love [for God]? It is that a person should love God with an exceedingly great and powerful love to the point that his soul is bound up with the love of God. He is continually obsessed by it, as if he were smitten by lovesickness. [Divine love can be understood from a man's love for a woman], for he cannot take his mind off his love for that woman, and is continually obsessed by her, whether he is sitting or standing, eating or drinking . . . This is what King Solomon stated in parable form: "For I am sick with love" (*Song of Songs* 2:5).

Rabbi Akiva, you will recall, was the author of the earliest recorded kabbalistic text and the preeminent master of the early second-century rabbinic tradition. His relationship with his wife is one of the finest examples of love in the Jewish tradition. Listen to what he says about the union of man and woman: The Hebrew word for man is *ish*. It consists of the three Hebrew letters *aleph, yud,* and *shin*. The Hebrew word for woman is *ishah* and is made up of the Hebrew letters *aleph, shin,* and *hay.* The words *ish* and *ishah* share the Hebrew letters *aleph* and *shin*. These letters also make up the word *esh* (fire). But the Hebrew words *ish* and *ishah* each have a letter that the other lacks. *Ish* has a *yud* and *ishah* has a *hay.* The letters *yud* and *hay,* in turn, make up the word *Yah*. This is one of the names of God.

Rabbi Akiva pointed out that the words *ish* and *ishah* and the permutations of their letters teach a profound lesson. When husband and wife are united in pure, fulfilling love, *ish* and *ishah* bring God's presence into the relationship, enveloping themselves in the *Shekhinah.* This is the function of *Yesod,* which opens the couple to the Divine, and causes holy energy to flow into the world. However, when sexual relations do not express committed love, God is absent. *Ish* and *ishah* without the *yud* and the *hay* are merely a momentary flash of *esh,* and there is nothing beyond ephemeral passion. When the flame fizzles, cold and darkness remain. Worse, fire burns. Passion without love can consume the lovers. As you read in chapter 6, loving sex between husband and wife consummates their relationship. Without love, sex may consume and destroy it. The *esh* quality of love, its burnout or fizzle, often characterizes sexual relationships, reflecting imbalance in *Netzach, Hod,* and, especially, *Yesod.* This is what happened to Rachel and David.

RACHEL AND DAVID'S STORY

Couples who adhere to Jewish law refrain from physical intimacy both during menstruation and for several days after all bleeding has stopped. Rachel began to telephone me anonymously about resuming intimacy, but always called well after the usual period of separation had passed. I was troubled by her unenthusiastic response whenever I told her that there were no religious impediments to resuming conjugal relations, and so I suggested that she consult a marriage and family therapist. She decided to shed her anonymity and told me that she and her husband attended services at my synagogue. At our first meeting, she revealed that she had never previously consulted a rabbi about intimate matters. Instead, she had simply delayed preparing herself for the monthly resumption of intimacy with her husband.

Rachel had received numerous explicit and subliminal messages about the ugliness and unholiness of sex from her mother and the teachers in her religious school. Moreover, the woman to whom she had gone for premarital instruction had told her that if her mouth ever made contact with her husband's genitals, her prayers would never again be answered. Rachel was convinced that sexual intercourse was merely a necessary and painful part of the marital contract, intended solely for reproduction, and, within strict parameters, for her husband's sexual release. It was not surprising that she had come to believe that her strategies for delaying the monthly resumption of intercourse reflected her deep piety rather than her issues about sexuality.

David was an only son whose parents had been divorced early in his life. His father had moved across the country and initially saw him for no more than two or three weeks a year. Eventually, even these visits were terminated by his neurotic stepmother. David's pain was compounded by his mother's love life. She had married and divorced twice more and had had a succession of live-in lovers. David suffered disappointment when each new man in his mother's life left. When he was a teenager he was particularly wounded by one breakup. His mother had become involved with a man whom David came to regard as the father for whom he had always longed, who helped him with his homework and did fun things with him. But something prevented him from marrying David's mother, causing David the constant worry that this special person would also walk out on them. His mother finally delivered her ultimatum: "Marry me or stop seeing us." He chose the latter.

From these experiences, David learned that people you love will leave if anything goes wrong. Although he realized that his mother must have made some errors, he was also troubled by the possibility that he himself had been an unwitting cause of some of the breakups. As a result, he decided to hold on to important relationships, regardless of the psychological cost. His relationship with Rachel was deeply conflicted. He could not openly fault her for placing limitations on their intimacy, because her piety was one of the reasons he had been attracted to her. Since she was deeply principled, came from a solid family, and was loyal to God, he was certain she would be loyal to him also. But their lovemaking was infrequent and unfulfilling. David's head and heart were not in sync. Rationalizing his unfulfilling sexual relationship away had not prevented him from growing bitter and from resenting his wife and her religious values.

I agreed to meet with Rachel and David for a short series of sessions on the religious and spiritual dimensions of human sexuality, and then to refer them for specialized sex therapy.

The Meaning of Rachel and David's Story

Rachel had become defective on every *sefirah* level. Her spirituality was superficial and mechanical, and her relationship with the Divine was based on fear rather than love. Even her knowledge of her own religious practices was grossly inadequate. Her *Sefirot* of emotion and relationships were as out of balance as her *Sefirot* of cognition. Rachel had learned to become all *Gevurah,* and so many things had become off limits to her. She was austere and self-sacrificing, neither fully able to receive her husband's love nor give him the love he needed. Her *Chesed* was underdeveloped, and her *Da'at* atrophied. She could not permit herself to let her husband truly know her the way Adam had known his Eve. She had not allowed him to strip away her persona and *kelipot.* Her *Tif'eret,* too, was undeveloped. She had had no authentic experience of beauty and harmony in her intimate relationships with her husband. Just as her *Gevurah* was overdeveloped, so, too, was her *Hod.* She recoiled from truly embracing David and had reduced herself to an object for his occasional sexual release. Her own sexual needs were deeply repressed, and the dance of giving and receiving between partners was absent. In addition, she had disowned her *Netzach,* and failed to develop her *Yesod.*

For his part, David was all *Hod.* His life strategy had stunted his *Netzach,* and he had sacrificed his own emotional needs to maintain his marriage. He, too, did not know how to give love, and he was terrified of losing his wife's love. His *Sefirot* were just as out of balance as Rachel's. Their sexual dysfunction pointed to problems on every other *sefirah* level.

Spiritual Interventions

◉ *Reeducation: Bibliotherapy.* I provided Rachel and David with a list of inspirational readings on the Jewish attitude to marital intimacy. Included on my list were Norman Lamm's *A Hedge of Roses;* chapters 3, 4, and 5 of David M. Feldman's *Marital Relations, Birth Control and Abortion in Jewish Law;* and Aharon Feldman's *The River, the Kettle and the Bird.* I strongly recommended that they read *The Holy Letter,* translated and with an introduction by Seymour J. Cohen. This thirteenth-century treatise on the sex life of husband and wife had long been ascribed to the great kabbalistic master Moses Nachmanides. It was, however, probably written by Joseph Gikatilla, who died in about the year 1325 and was a younger contemporary of Nachmanides and a member of his kabbalistic circle. I drew David and Rachel's attention to a number of key passages in this inspiring little book.

> Know that the union of man with his wife is divided into two parts. Know that the sexual intercourse of man with his wife is holy and pure when done properly, in the proper time with the proper intention. No one should think that sexual intercourse is ugly and loathsome, God forbid. (p. 72)

> I should remind you in addition of a great principle of the Torah: the masters of blessed memory said, when a man and a wife are pure in intention and both intend the act for the sake of goodness, God joins with them. (p. 146)

> Therefore, when engaging in the sex act, you must begin by speaking to her in a manner that will draw her heart to you, calm her spirits and make her happy. Thus, your minds will be

bound upon one another as one, and your intention will unite with hers. Speak to her so that your words will provoke desire, love, will and passion as well as words leading to reverence for God, piety and modesty. (p. 172)

Therefore, a husband should speak with his wife with the appropriate words, some of erotic passion, some words of fear of the Lord. (p. 174)

A man should never force himself upon his wife and never overpower her, for the Divine Spirit never rests upon one whose conjugal relations occur in the absence of desire, love and free will. The *Shekhinah* does not rest there . . . The Talmud (*Pasachim* 49b) tells us that just as a lion tears at its prey and eats it shamelessly, so does an ignorant man strike and sleep with his wife. Rather act so that you will warm her heart by speaking to her charming and seductive words. (pp. 174–176)

To conclude, when you are ready for sexual union, see that your wife's intentions combine with yours. Do not hurry to arouse her until she is receptive. Be calm, and, as you enter the path of love and will, let her insemination [sexual arousal] come first. (p. 176)

⊙ *Reeducation: Instruction in Jewish Marital Law.* We also studied the Jewish legal texts that defined the parameters of permissible marital sexual encounters. Given what Rachel had heard from her teacher before marriage, we paid special attention to Maimonides' normative ruling in *Mishneh Torah: Hilkhot Isurei Biah [Laws of Illicit Intercourse]*.

For a man's wife is permitted to him; therefore . . . they may have intercourse at any time they wish . . . he may be joined to her in the usual manner or have sexual congress of other kinds, as long as he does not bring forth seed in vain. However, it is a sign of piety not to show too much levity, but to sanctify himself at the time of intercourse. (21:10)

I referred Rachel to a sensitive teacher, the wife of a rabbinic colleague, for a review of the laws of Jewish marital purity. This woman enjoyed a good reputation, both for her knowledge of the law and her openness to the concerns of modern young women. I referred David to a rabbinic colleague who was giving husbands a refresher course on the laws of Jewish family purity. I was confident that both teachers would project the magic, beauty, and poetry of sexual intimacy without compromising Jewish law.

⦿ *Referrals.* Effective sex therapy should take account of the entire psychospiritual makeup of the couple. It should relate to their cognitive, emotional, and relational needs as well as to techniques for achieving arousal and satisfying physical union. In *The Illustrated Manual of Sex Therapy,* Dr. Helen Singer Kaplan describes her approach as follows:

> The beauty of this method of sex therapy lies in combining structured sexual interactions with psychotherapy. In actual practice *most* of the therapist's activities are psychotherapeutic and consist of active interpretation, support, clarification and integration of the experiences with the couple in the office sessions. This dynamic interplay between experience and psychotherapy constitutes the essence of the new sex therapy. (p. 169)

I also recommend another of Dr. Kaplan's books, *The Evaluation of Sexual Disorders: Psychological and Medical Aspects.* Because Dr. Kaplan's approach to sex therapy is more holistic than most, I limited my referral list to expert practitioners of this method.

⦿ *Marital Prayer and Meditation.* I recorded the following prayer and meditation for Rachel and David, which is included on my meditation CD.

MARITAL PRAYER AND MEDITATION

Before making love, husband and wife may sit together, holding hands, and recite the following prayer.

O Lord, our God, Master of the Universe and Source of all love, cause your *Shekhinah* to envelop us. Keep us safe and secure in the *Shekhinah's* embrace. Open our minds and heart to your loving energy. Let us be surrounded by your light. Transform our love into an act of union with you, as well as with each other. Grant us the gift of self-transcendence. Help us connect to our higher selves. Transmute our passion into an energy that extends beyond ourselves to the farthest reaches of the cosmos. Permit us to witness your love in our love, and your light through our light. Make our act of union a conduit to holiness and wholeness. Make our oneness with each other and in each other an intimation of your at-one-ness with all Creation. Allow our joining to become a deep knowing. Grant us the primal experience of Adam and Eve, of whom it was said: "And Adam knew his wife . . . and they became one flesh."

We give thanks to you for your gift of love. We are grateful beyond the telling for the wondrous way in which you have fashioned us, allowing us pleasure and joy, permitting us intimacy and ecstasy, enabling us to experience the joy of our physicality, ever aware that our physical joining is a bridge to the Infinite.

Blessed are you, who made us in your image. Blessed are you, for your gift of love and for the wonders of our union as husband and wife. Blessed are you for having created us male and female, two halves that can become one whole.

Following the recitation of this prayer, or any other that comes to mind, sit comfortably together and prepare to meditate.

1. Allow yourselves to be aware of your bodies on the chair. Feel your weight.
2. Place your hands palms up on your lap and inhale deeply. After each inhalation, hold your breath for a count of five. Exhale, mindful of your breath. Repeat four times.
3. After the fifth inhalation and exhalation, inhale deeply,

filling your diaphragm, and feeling tension leave your body as you exhale.

4. Fill your heart with loving thoughts about each other. Stay with these thoughts awhile. Imagine your love as light that fills your heart. Now allow this light of love to rise from your heart to your head. Feel your love. Know your love. Experience your light. Then allow your love and light to ascend above your head, three, six, or sixty-seven feet. Remain there with your love. Witness your love. Know that you have moved from alpha to theta brain-wave rhythms and that you are ready to receive the energies of God.

5. Imagine that you are bathed in golden light. Feel its warmth and loving caress. Allow some of that light to enter your crown. Be aware of your connection to that light. Let it wash away the tensions in your head, relaxing your eyes, cheeks, mouth, and jaw. Know that you have opened your *Chochmah,* creating a perfect channel for divine energy and inspiration.

6. Allow the light to pass into your neck, washing away tension and relaxing your neck muscles. Witness the light pass into your shoulders, relaxing them, and from your shoulders into your upper arms, your elbows, your forearms, your wrists, and your hands. Allow the light to pass through your fingers, rejoining the soothing golden light that envelops you.

7. Now allow the light from your head and neck to pass into your chest, relaxing your heart and lungs, and cleansing your inner organs.

8. See the light of love in your heart grow brighter, suffusing your entire upper body, pouring through your skin into the light that surrounds you. Your *Chesed* channel is opening wider and wider. The power of your love cleanses and relaxes you.

9. Allow the light to move from your trunk through your waist, relaxing and bathing your organs of reproduction and your

legs, opening your *Netzach, Hod,* and *Yesod.* You are suffused with love. You are love.

10. Witness the light as it passes through your hips to your thighs. Feel it relax your thigh muscles. The light is now moving through your knees into your legs, relaxing the muscles of your calves. Witness the light as it passes through your ankles into your feet, washing the final vestiges of tension from your body. Be aware of the light passing through your feet into the ground.

11. Know that the light that expands within your body is one with the golden light that surrounds you.

12. You are deeply relaxed. Relaxed and at ease. Your eyelids feel heavier. Be aware of the tranquillity and peacefulness that surround you and embrace you.

13. Imagine yourself transported together to a place of ethereal beauty. Picture yourself floating above your body, gently moving through the air, aware of the miracles of God's Creation below you and above you.

14. Feel yourself descending slowly into a beautiful garden. Hear the rustle of the leaves. Inhale the fragrance of the flowers in your garden. Listen to the songs of the birds. This is your Garden of Eden. Sit down on the grass and enjoy it all.

15. You are Adam and Eve, the first human beings, the first lovers. Know that like Adam and Eve, you are one soul split into two. Like Adam and Eve, the halves have come together. The jigsaw puzzle pieces are joined. You are one. You are also at one with the Infinite.

16. Remain in your garden. Become aware of each other's light and loving energy. Enjoy the light of the *Shekhinah* as it surrounds you. Experience its tranquillity. Stay in this awareness for a few minutes. Linger together in your primordial garden. Know that the spiritual togetherness you are experiencing will soon be consummated by the joy of physical union. Know that your joining will be pure and pleasur-

able, an expression of your passion and poetry, and that this is a springboard to the deepest mysteries of the universe. Stay with these thoughts. Enjoy the light within. Enjoy the light without. Witness your separate lights intermingle and become one brilliant, radiant illumination.

17. When you are ready, slowly open your eyes. Touch each other and prepare to become one flesh.

14

REBALANCING OUR *SEFIRAH*
OF *MALCHUT*

——◆◆◆——

You will recall that *Malchut* governs our earthly domain, the realm of *Asiyah*. It is here that the intimate association of two people expands into family, community, and polity. The way we live in these collectives obviously affects our society and our world. Less obvious is its transcendent influence. *Malchut* is the feedback mechanism of the entire *sefirah* system. The holy energies it generates are transmitted back to the Source of all being and become the engine for cosmic *tikkun*. To the extent that we succeed in establishing the kingdom of God on earth, it is also established in all universes, both visible and invisible. The challenge for humankind is the eradication of evil by societies, states, and international organizations. The project is huge, but since all human collectives begin with the family, the challenge is manageable. The healthy family is the key to the entire process, for it is uniquely structured for the implementation of the cosmic *tikkun*.

COSMIC *TIKKUN*

The second *Mishnah* in *Avot (Ethics of the Fathers)* states: "Simon the Just was [one] of the surviving members of the Great Assembly. He used to say: 'The world stands on three things—on the Torah, on divine service, and on acts of loving-kindness.' " Even at first blush, the meaning of two parts of Simon's statement make eminent sense. The Torah is the blueprint of civilization, mandating the behavior of members of a just society and establishing the moral imperatives that govern relationships between individuals. It provides for the management of disputes between individuals and groups and between various groupings within society, legislates the morality of warfare, and spells out the conditions for peaceful co-existence. Clearly, absent these principles and imperatives, the law of the jungle prevails. This is why Simon the Just insists that the survival of the world depends upon the Torah.

Simon's second point is also unproblematic, because worshipping God raises our consciousness of our dependence upon him for our continued existence and leads to behavior affirming our creatureliness. However, his third point is more difficult to understand. How do acts of loving-kindness between individuals affect the entire world? To be sure, individual acts of benevolence have an impact on the lives of others. But what has this to do with the Divine and the survival of the world as a whole?

Rabbi Judah Loewe of Prague answered this question in his comment on a parable from the Zohar. Imagine a source of living waters emerging as a river. The river flows through many towns, irrigating their farms. Its tributaries fertilize fields located even farther from the source, providing sustenance to a great many people. Streams flow through distant farmlands and, in turn, fertilize many other fields. But then a selfish farmer decides to prevent the waters from flowing beyond his boundaries. He builds a dam, thinking that he alone will be assured of rich harvests and profitable markets, and that those who are cut off from the water will lose their crops and be obliged to purchase his produce. At first, his plan works well. The stream overflows into his fields and the vegetation on his property becomes lusher and lusher. His land yields more and more, but, ultimately, his selfish strategy backfires. The water behind his dam becomes stagnant, a breeding place for mosquitoes and disease, and his crops begin to wither and die.

According to Rabbi Loewe, God is the Source to which the parable alludes. The divine overflow is continuous only as long as its benefits are distributed farther and farther afield. Once the divine grace is blocked, and the divine goodness dammed up by selfish individuals, the critical mass of godness in the world is diminished. Initially, only those from whom his blessings are withheld feel the impact, but, eventually, even those who have kept the bounty to themselves suffer the effects of stagnation, disease, and disintegration.

Individual acts of loving-kindness are conduits for the Divine. When the bounty is not shared and goodness is not distributed, the Divine is withheld from the world. When we fail to act as conduits for *Havayah,* the world is in danger of losing its *havayah.* The psalmist did not exaggerate when he declared, "The [entire] world is built on loving-kindness" (Ps. 59:3).

The Kabbalah offers an even deeper analysis of Simon the Just's statement. One of the primary functions of *Tif'eret* is the revelation of the Torah. Our study of the Torah pulls powerful *Tif'eret* energy into our individual, family, and community lives. The surge of this energy from above awakens latent divine energies in our world, reversing the flow, transmitting increased energy back through the *Sefirot,* mending shattered vessels, eliminating evil, and bringing those who study the Torah closer to its Source and their Higher Selves. It is in this sense that the study of the Torah sustains the world. Prayer and meditation also stir up awakenings from below, releasing the spiritual energies of the individuals engaged in worship. This new collective awakening brings about the union of the *Shekhinah* in the world of *Asiyah* with the supernal *Sefirot* of *Chesed, Gevurah, Tif'eret, Netzach, Hod,* and *Yesod.* Human benevolence has the same cosmic effect. The Kabbalah puts it this way: Worship and benevolence bring about the union of the feminine divine energy in our world with the masculine supernal energies beyond. The result of the fusion of these energies is the awakening of a great illumination of *Chesed.* The resulting flow of even more powerful *Chesed* energies to our world mitigates harsh judgments against us, enabling us to continue to enjoy *havayah* despite our shortcomings. This is the deeper meaning of the Zohar's parable and the third part of Simon the Just's statement. Individual, familial, and societal acts of *chesed* are responsible for attracting supernal *Chesed,* thus maintaining *Havayah* in the world, and enabling its continued existence.

THE ROLE OF FAMILY AND COMMUNITY

Up to now, I've described the rebalancing of the *Sefirot* of individuals, each of whom is a microcosm. The macrocosm is made up of families, communities, societies, nations, the world, and the cosmos as a whole. A family whose *Sefirot* are in balance is the smallest unit of the macrocosm. Its healthy and spiritually meaningful functioning determines the health of the community and the larger social structures of which it is a part. Therefore, healing the broken structures of the family and rebalancing its *Sefirot* have a profound impact on the larger collectives and, ultimately, the entire cosmos.

Families often suffer from the *sefirah* dysfunction we have seen in individuals, but in a more complex way. The bad news is that the family is a system, and dysfunction in one part of the system affects the whole. Some of the stories I have shared are good examples of this. The narcissistic woman to whom you were introduced in chapter 13 influenced the attitudes and behaviors of her husband and children. The waves she created rippled and sometimes roared through the whole family. But this is not confined to the nuclear family: It is transgenerational, impacting the lives of people who marry into the family and affecting the children of coming generations. Ilana was abused by the narcissistic strategies that Max had learned from his mother, and was getting ready to leave him. Their children were terrified at the prospect of an impending divorce, and one of the children became ill, giving them a shared project in an attempt to keep their parents together. Since the child's asthma was the transgenerational effect of her grandmother's narcissism, her psychologists called her the carrier of the family pathology.

However, the fact that the family is an interlocking, interdependent system is also very good news, because a positive change in one part of the family's system will also affect the entire family. Max's behavior began to change when he accepted responsibility and took steps to grow spiritually and psychologically. When this happened, Ilana joined him in therapy, and as she grew with her husband, her own *Sefirot* gradually came into alignment. Their daughter's asthma began to clear up as the family became happier, safer, and a source of shared inspiration and optimism.

Though the principle of the family as an interlocking system does not change, sometimes the process is much more complicated. The tale I'm about to share makes this point.

THE BERMAN FAMILY'S STORY

Ten-year-old Michael Berman was referred to me several months after the Northridge earthquake. From the time of the temblor, he refused to sleep in his own room, began to wet his bed, washed his hands compulsively thirty or forty times a day, would not wear tight-fitting clothes or even underwear for fear of infection, failed at school, and regularly beat up his seven-year-old sister, Geraldine.

Our first two sessions went nowhere. Michael sat on his chair, knees against his chest, shirt pulled over his head and knees, and refused to talk. To break the impasse, I asked his parents, Harrison and Gloria, to accompany him to our third meeting. More relaxed with his parents present, Michael played games with me that were designed to reveal children's inner lives. His responses led me to believe that he was more frightened of fault lines running through his family than he was of further earthquake damage to his house.

I met with Harrison and Gloria for a couples session a few days later. He was a good-looking forty-three-year-old, but she was obese and unkempt. When I voiced my opinion about the deeper meaning of Michael's earthquake phobia, the Bermans admitted that their marriage was in trouble and that their son was the shared problem that was keeping them together. But Michael was not the only carrier of the family pathology. Gerry had begun to soil her pajamas and was having an increasing number of embarrassing "accidents" at school. Her frequent absences from class had led to numerous, unproductive meetings with her teacher and the school nurse, and the family physician could find no medical reason for her problem.

Fifteen-year-old Stanley was also troubled. His highest grade was a D. He bullied other children and excelled only at football. Michael and Gerry dealt with his rage by keeping their distance.

During the course of several subsequent couples sessions, I learned that as a child and a teen, Gloria had been regularly sexually abused by her stepfather. She tearfully disclosed her fear of sexual intimacy and admitted that she had begun to gain weight and neglect her appearance shortly after Gerry was born as a way of becoming sexually undesirable. Gloria's disclosure of her stepfather's behavior was news to Harrison and made sense of her obesity, unattractive attire, and emotional distance. He was visibly moved by her vulnerability and the pathos of her situation.

The Meaning of the Berman Family's Story

Like Susannah, Gloria believed that she was dirty and ugly and that people were not to be trusted; but unlike Susannah, her strategy was to create the family she had never had, while simultaneously keeping herself safe from further sexual exploitation. She had married a good man but alienated his affections. She wanted her children to receive the kind of love she had never known, but they had all become ill, and too absorbed with their problems to appreciate her attempts to get close to them.

Gloria's situation reflected her radically unbalanced *sefirah* system. She had resisted falling into the dysfunctional *Hod* trap by maintaining emotional distance, but had, in the process, become a personification of *Gevurah* imbalance, with defensive walls of dowdy clothing and fatty tissue. By overprotecting herself, she had allowed her *Chesed* to atrophy in tandem with her neglected *Yesod* energies.

Each Berman child carried the symptoms of the marital pathology differently. Gerry reverted to infantile behavior, enduring public embarrassment to keep Mom and Dad together, and, in doing so, came to personify the dark side of *Hod*. Michael's obsessive-compulsive behaviors were symptomatic of his immature *Gevurah* defenses. His attacks on little Gerry reflected the shadow side of his *Gevurah*, while his dark *Hod* explained his regressive bed-wetting, since he was prepared to suffer the embarrassment of wetting himself and the burden of his compulsive behaviors to keep his mom and dad together. Stanley, in turn, was all *Gevurah*, defending himself with unprovoked attacks on others, his *Sefirot* of cognition almost entirely blocked.

The Berman family was a classic example of systemic *sefirah* dysfunction.

Interventions

Empty chair and reparenting techniques helped Gloria deal with her childhood issues. The family as a whole benefited from the following therapeutic strategies.

- ◉ *Couples Therapy.* Gloria's continued revelations about her experience of abuse cleared up many issues for Harrison. His sensitivity to the horror of her childhood made it easier for her to succeed at Weight Watchers and keep weekly appointments at the beauty parlor and manicurist. Harrison rewarded her weight loss by getting her new outfits and agreed to surprise her with an interesting place or event for their weekly date together. They responded very well to Helen Singer Kaplan's sensate focusing techniques, journaling their interactions as the focus of further therapeutic discussion. We agreed that it was not appropriate for them to discuss Gloria's experience of sexual abuse with the children, but if the kids did raise the issue of sexual abuse during family therapy sessions, Gloria would answer honestly, without giving any details.
- ◉ *Family Therapy.* The following technique was used.
  - • *Facilitation of Open Communication.* The basic ground rule for communication during sessions was openness and respect. Everybody would be encouraged to respond to what was said, but rudeness and bullying would not be tolerated. Harrison and Gloria would establish their firm but open leadership of the family. The objective was not only democratic and honest conversation, but also mod-

eling respect and sensitivity—especially since many raw nerves would be exposed.

The opening session began with the discussion of the state of the marriage, because the fragility of Harrison and Gloria's relationship had been the invisible "eight-hundred-pound gorilla" in their home. At the first session, I asked Harrison to open the discussion. He responded with great sensitivity, acknowledging the serious problems he and Gloria had been having, their fighting, and his frequent threats to walk out. Gloria took her share of responsibility for what had happened between them, mentioning that she had deliberately become fat to be unattractive to her husband. Stanley asked why she had done this, and she replied that she had had a tough childhood and was frightened of getting too close to any male, even her husband. Stanley asked her outright, "Were you abused as a kid?" Gloria began to cry, and Harrison put his arm around her. I asked whether any of the children had questions about what they had heard. Nobody asked for details.

Michael wanted to know if things were going to be better between his parents. They told him that things were already much better, that Mom was working on losing weight and taking care of herself, and that she and Dad were going to have private time away from home one evening a week. When the younger kids protested that they'd feel left out, it was decided to make Sunday a family day. Geraldine wanted to know if Dad was still going to leave. He told her that he and Mom were doing all these things so that they could stay together for many, many years.

The conversation was gently shifted to the sibling concerns. Gerry complained that Michael kept beating her up, and they both complained that Stanley was a bully who forced them to do things they didn't want to do. When Stanley began to mock his brother's bed-wetting and his sister's soiling, Harrison reminded him that he was not perfect either, and that he should improve himself before putting others down. We agreed to spend much of each subsequent meeting in free and open conversation. Harrison and Gloria were encouraged to adopt a zero-tolerance policy to some of the pushing and shoving that occasionally happened during family exchanges and begin to insist that the children use words rather than force.

- *In-Home Session.* I scheduled the second session at their home. The kitchen sink was piled high with dirty dishes and clothes and shoes littered the floor, reflecting the chaos in the family's relationships. Gloria apologized and said she was overwhelmed by having to get the kids off to school in the morning, because they didn't get up in time to help her. There was a great deal of discussion about this, and eventually, the children said they would try to make things easier for her.

- *Reinforcement Schedule.* The major part of our third session was devoted to developing a daily schedule for each of the children. Every item on the schedule was associated with a reward. The family would grade the children on their noncompletion, partial completion, or total completion of tasks, such as getting up on time, washing up, making their beds, tidying their rooms, getting their things together for school, dishwashing, caring for pets, and doing their homework. In addition, goals were set for the extinction of dysfunctional behaviors. Michael would receive points for a reduction in daily hand washings, attacks on Gerry, and bed-wettings, and bonus points for nights spent in his own bedroom and wearing underwear. Gerry received points for each day and night she kept herself clean, and other tasks and challenges were added to equalize her possible point totals with Michael's. Stanley would receive points for improvement in his grades and a reduction of his aggressive behaviors both at school and at home. His homeroom teacher would allocate weekly points for his schoolwork and social interactions at school. The family would assign points for each day at home that passed without his physically abusing his siblings. Gloria agreed to make three charts and post them in the kitchen. The children would receive rewards based on their scores, and the nature of the rewards would be determined by the whole family at therapy sessions.

⊙ *Spiritual Interventions.* The Bermans had not been synagogue-goers, but now they undertook to worship together once a week and to attend weekly Torah classes. Michael and Geraldine were enrolled in the community religious school. Their synagogue was a sponsor of **Tomchei Shabbos,** a program that supplies meals for indigent members of the community. When Harrison came home from work on Thursday afternoons, the children accompanied him to the central food preparation depot, where Stanley, Michael, and Geraldine helped pack food baskets and then drove with their dad to homes, where they placed the baskets by the doors. The program was intended to be anonymous, since anonymous benevolence is the highest act of *Chesed.* Occasionally, however, an elderly resident would see the children coming and greet them. This way, Stanley, Michael, and Geraldine came to know people from a different generation and in very different economic circumstances. They maintained contact with some, developing friendships and calling during the week. The children's introduction to political activism was a letter-writing campaign to the president, key senators, and congressmen on a burning international issue. To their surprise, they received replies, and in this way discovered that individuals, families, and communities can play a role, even on the international level. The Berman family's *Chesed* and *Netzach,* so neglected during the period of family dysfunction, had begun to repair.

⊙ *Intermittent Reinforcement.* Many studies have shown the efficacy of behavior modification techniques through regular and frequent reinforcement. However, relapse often occurs in the absence of subsequent intermittent reinforcement. After the issues had been resolved, I continued the therapy on a less frequent and more irregular schedule.

The Berman family met for family therapy once a week for a full year. The open discussions proved to be very effective. Michael learned to speak his mind clearly and respectfully. His dysfunctional *Hod* characteristics had been replaced by healthy *Gevurah* tendencies. His readiness to defend Geraldine when neighborhood kids reminded her of her soiling problem showed healthy *Chesed, Gevurah,* and *Netzach* characteristics. Michael's bed-wetting, obsessive-compulsive behaviors, violence, and anxiety about infection and death gradually left him. Geraldine had fewer and fewer accidents. Stanley's grades improved, and the former schoolyard bully came to be admired not only for his prowess on the football field, but also for his concern for his classmates.

By year's end, Gloria had lost more than a hundred pounds and took pride in her appearance. She and Harrison often held hands in family therapy sessions. The improvement in their relationship was probably as much a factor in the extinction of the children's dysfunctional behaviors as the reinforcement schedule had been. The family's participation in their community and their new experience of spirituality had turned them into a unit that did things for one another and for others. The family system as a whole had been reenergized by rebalancing its *Sefirot* and its openness to the Divine.

15

AFTER *SEFIRAH* REBALANCING:
FROM HEALING TO GROWTH

—◀◈▶—

SPIRITUAL EMERGENCY,
SPIRITUAL EMERGENCE

The seminar was in the afternoon of its second day. During small group breakout sessions, participants had already come to understand their strategies for success. Many had taken the microphone and spoken of their unhappiness and their habit of blaming others for what they had become. Some had publicly explored what they could do to accept personal responsibility for their lives. They had all role-played the completion process and described their actual experiences of completion. The seminar consisted of alternating sessions on the psychology of the Kabbalah and group process. The group discussions enabled the participants to learn how to integrate kabbalistic psychological principles into their lives.

In psychological literature, the layers of armor that we wear are often called masks or personae—what we call our personalities. The fact that those who know us can so accurately describe us in terms of our strategies for success shows just how effective our masks are. But they conceal far more than they reveal. This is why authentic relationships can develop only when both people take off their masks. We do not trust acquaintances enough to disclose our weaknesses and vulnerabilities, keeping our masks firmly in place. With friends, we lift our masks a little. We lift them even more with intimate friends, who, we believe, will not hurt us, and who have risked dropping their own defenses to allow us in. We permit soul mates to look into our very souls, to know our essence, because we feel no need to hide from people we love completely. We are confident they will love us no matter how we are, and keep us safe, nurturing us in our neediness, and protecting us from the things that make us feel vulnerable.

But what happens if we use our masks to hide our essence from ourselves? What if our defensive layers are so dense that we cannot, or will not, pry them loose? What happens when we have become as taken in by our strategies as other people? These questions can be reframed in kabbalistic terms: How do we get to know our true selves after we have spent a lifetime covering ourselves in *kelipot?*

It was, as I said, the afternoon of the second day of the seminar. A young woman who was clearly agitated asked for the microphone. We already knew that she was a prominent television anchor. Her contributions in the groups and public sessions had been models of clarity and articulation. Her clothes were stylish, and her face and hair perfect. Obviously, she took her appearance seriously.

"What do you mean when you say that our personae conceal who we really are?" she asked. "I know who I am. I'm the person I see in the mirror every day. I'm the person that anyone who watches my show knows. What you see is what you get. The true me is exactly what you see. My personality is the person I am."

"Are you really the person you saw in the mirror this morning?" I asked.

"Of course. The mirror image of me is me."

I paused for just a moment. "Think back to another image of yourself. Tell us how you looked when you were fifteen. What did fifteen-year-old Doreen see in her mirror? Do you remember? Please be honest."

"Of course I looked different when I was fifteen. My hair, oh, yes, I may as well say it, wasn't blonde. I had braces on my teeth. My face was covered in pimples and my glasses made me look terrible. And, yes, I was fat and ugly. I hated looking in the mirror. Obviously, I didn't look the way I do now. I've worked very hard at becoming the woman I see in the mirror nowadays. What are you getting at?"

"Do you remember what you saw in the mirror when you were ten years old?"

"In fact, I do. My teeth were very crooked, my glasses were ugly, and I was short for my age. I remember envying my girlfriends who were so much prettier than I. Some of them had even begun to get curves, but I was just like a little boy in girl's clothes."

"Doreen, I'm sure you've seen pictures of yourself as a baby. Think of who you were then. You had tiny fingers, little legs and arms, a small body, and a very different-looking face. Right?"

"Of course. But so what? What's this to do with my personality and my real self?"

"Everything. Which image is your real self? The baby you remember from your pictures? The ten-year-old who looked like a little boy? The fifteen-year-old who thought she was fat and ugly? Or the beautiful, competent, perfectly attired anchor who is holding the microphone at this moment and looked at herself in the mirror this morning? Doreen, which you is really you? Your body has changed in so many ways over the years. I know that you'll always be beautiful, but your body will continue to change. Will the sixty-year-old Doreen looking in the mirror one day be the same as the Doreen of today or the fifteen-year-old, ten-year-old, or one-year-old Doreen? My point is that you're not your body. Our bodies constantly change, but our essence remains. Our souls use our bodies to accomplish their mission, but they are not our bodies, and they are not the masks we put on for other people."

Doreen was upset. "If I'm not who I appear to be, who am I? Have I really constructed a person who is different from my true self?"

"Maybe it's easier for you not to know. Perhaps you're happy just the way you are. Lifting the veil, removing your mask, may be too tough."

A shadow passed over Doreen's face as she tried to hold her tears back, but then she began to sob. Someone moved to put her arm around her shoulders, but Doreen regained her composure, and spoke through her tears.

"You know I'm not happy with who I am. That's why I signed up for this course. Do you think I've not pictured myself as an older woman, and wondered whether my fans would remain loyal? Do you think my public success makes up for my personal failures? How do you think a woman feels who has been unable to sustain her marriages? I know that my inside and my outside are not the same, but I'm terrified of looking in and finding what I will find. No one knows my nagging doubts about myself. Nobody knows how much I fear being exposed as insecure, vulnerable, and frightened. Maybe I'm better off thinking I am the person in the mirror."

Doreen had taken the risk of publicly acknowledging her self-doubt, and in this way, admitting that her personae were fashioned from *kelipot*.

Psychiatrist Stanislav Grof distinguished between spiritual emergency and spiritual emergence. Spiritual emergency is the disorganization and bewilderment we experience when we look into the abyss and discover that we have lived inauthentically. Spiritual emergence is the beginning of our quest to discover who we are. Sometimes spiritual emergency and spiritual emergence converge. At the moment we face our inauthenticity, we begin our journey to authentic being. Doreen was experiencing such a moment. She acknowledged the emptiness of her personality and contemplated shattering her armor to find the person who had been hiding deep inside. Like so many other participants in the group, she was preparing to move from healing to wholeness.

FROM HEALING TO WHOLENESS

Dr. Levi Meier, a rabbinic friend and colleague, taught me the difference between curing and healing. His work as head of the chaplaincy department in a large hospital had convinced him that they were not the same. Many patients in his hospital had incurable illnesses, but he was able to help them make peace with their situation and find answers to difficult questions. He guided them in their transition from life this side of the grave to life beyond, as they completed unfinished business with their loved ones, mending family rifts, and sharing the dreams they cherished for their children and children's children. This often calmed them, and although they had not been cured, they had been healed.

Kabbalistic psychology goes a step further and distinguishes between healing and wholeness. Rebalancing our *Sefirot* brings healing and the end of dysfunction. But wholeness is far more than spiritual homeostasis. People need to do more than merely regain and maintain their spiritual balance. Wholeness is spiritual growth. It starts with self-discovery, moving rebalanced *Sefirot* to higher levels, and nurturing the Godness that resides, sometimes deeply hidden, in every human being.

FINDING OUR CALLING

Doreen had asked what she would find beneath her defensive layers. I'd told her that she'd find herself if she were ready to take the risk. What did I mean? The Talmud, in a passage I cited on page 52, declares that before our birth, a light shines above our heads, illuminating the entire world and revealing everything we need to know. But then an angel taps us on our lips and a wave of forgetfulness washes over us. According to this text, all learning is discovering, uncovering, and remembering. The sages do not mean us to believe that every unborn child is familiar with the intricacies of quantum mechanics or biochemistry, but emphasize that even before we are born, we know the path we should be taking. However, we sometimes resist taking this path or are swept away by the changing currents of our lives.

This is the theme of James Hillman's *The Soul's Code: In Search of Character and Calling.* "Each person," he says, "enters the world called . . . A calling may be postponed, avoided, intermittently missed. It may also possess you completely. Whatever; eventually it will out. It makes its claim" (pp. 7–8). Hillman bases his hypothesis on the lived experience of remarkable people. Let me cite some of his examples.

An awkward sixteen-year-old appears on Amateur Night at the Harlem Opera House. She is scheduled to dance, and intends to dance. But when the emcee announces that the next competitor is a talented young dancer, she whispers in his ear that she's changed her mind and is going to sing. Instead of dancing, Ella Fitzgerald sang a song and gave three encores. How did she know that she was called to sing?

R. G. Collingwood (1889–1943) became one of the foremost

teachers of philosophy. One day, when he was eight years old, he was in his father's huge library. For no reason, he reached for a volume entitled *Kant's Theory of Ethics*. He didn't understand a word he read, but had a sense that he was holding a book containing things of utmost urgency, things that at all costs he had to understand. At that moment, he said, "I felt as if a veil had been lifted and my destiny revealed."

Yehudi Menuhin's parents frequently took him to concerts at London's Curran Theatre, and he became enthralled by the performance of first violinist Louis Persinger. He asked his parents to give him a violin for his fourth birthday, and arrange for Persinger to give him lessons. Instead, his parents bought him a toy violin, thinking his hands were too small to play a full-sized violin. He flung the toy violin to the floor.

Golda Meir was the prime minister who led Israel to victory in the 1973 Yom Kippur War. When she was eleven years old in her native Milwaukee, she organized a protest against the requirement that families must purchase their children's schoolbooks. The new ruling was not a problem for families like her own, but how were poor families to handle the additional burden? Little Golda rented a hall, assembled a committee, organized publicity, and marshaled community support. When her mother asked if she needed help in writing her speech, Golda replied, "I'll just say what's in my head." Her audience was swayed by her eloquence and reasoning, and the unfair requirement was soon dropped.

Do not be misled by the tales of these remarkable people. Ordinary people, whose stories are not well known, are just as capable of finding their calling. Let me share a few tales of my own with you.

Fairly early in my career, I had the good fortune to meet Sidney Lasman, a humble man who earned his living as a barber.

When we became better acquainted, he asked me if I'd be interested in seeing some of his paintings. They were stunning. One of them still hangs in my home. He had been blessed with great talent. Cutting hair was his livelihood, but not his life. He didn't need to sell his art. The fact that so many people he cared about displayed his canvases in their homes was reward enough.

Some years later, I got to know a remarkable woman. Ada Sharfman had been a great schoolteacher and was one of the most popular people in the community. Sadly, she was now suffering from cancer. One day, when I came to visit her, I noticed a cello in her living room. "I didn't know that you played the cello," I said.

"You couldn't because I didn't. All my life I've wanted to master this instrument but never had the time or opportunity. I can't work anymore, so, finally, I have the opportunity, and I'm grasping it with whatever strength remains."

How sad it was that she'd waited for a debilitating illness to open the doors of opportunity. How much richer her life would have been had she paused much earlier to answer this calling. She would have remained a great teacher, but she would also have added a dimension to her life and brought enormous joy to others.

MY PERSONAL TALE *(continued)*

I've already shared some of my story with you. Here's a little more. When I was a high school junior, I took an aptitude test, which was common in South Africa at the time, because students had to decide on a career path before entering college. I was convinced that I wanted to be an attorney. I was already a champion debater and on my way to winning the best speaker's award. At the vocational center, I figured out how to answer the questionnaire so that law would come out as my career path. A week later, the vocational guidance counselor told me that my responses had indicated that I should choose law as my profession, but that he'd like to get to know me a little better. So we had a freewheeling discussion for the next hour. Before he wished me luck and sent me on my way, he popped a strange question: "Have you ever considered the ministry as your calling?"

I was flabbergasted. I had not attended yeshiva and was not a fully observant Jew. In my wildest imaginings, I had never seen myself as a rabbi.

I answered his question firmly: "No. I know I'm cut out for law. The reason I came for this test was to persuade my family, and especially the people who grant college scholarships, that I'm making the right decision."

During my sophomore year at college, I began to have serious doubts about my decision. By the end of the year, I'd begun to consider teaching as my life work, and taught history and English to seniors in high school for a number of months.

During my junior year, my Hebrew professor, Dr. Louis I. Rabinowitz, the late chief rabbi of South Africa, asked me to remain behind after class. "Abner," he began, "what are you going to do for a living after graduating next year?"

I had not expected the question and had not given any consideration to what I was about to say. I blurted out, "I want to be a rabbi."

"You what?" he said. He paused, and the silence seemed to last forever. Finally, he said, "You mean a Reform rabbi."

I did not understand what he meant at the time because I didn't know enough. With hindsight, I can now fill in the blanks. The chief rabbi knew how little I knew about the Orthodox Jewish tradition, and that most candidates for the rabbinate had many years of training in rabbinic texts in elementary and high school. I was nearing the end of my college career and had never opened a volume of the Talmud. He also knew that I was a leader in a nonreligious Jewish youth movement. "No, sir, I don't want to be a Reform rabbi. I want to be an Orthodox rabbi."

He paused again and then said, "I'm sure you don't know that the leaders of the community have just decided to open South Africa's first training college for rabbis. I don't know if you can catch up, but you're welcome to try."

Without knowing why, I'd responded to a call for which I was ill prepared, at the precise moment that the first rabbinical school was about to open. How had the guidance counselor sensed that my career should be in religious leadership and not in law, in spite of the evidence to the contrary in my responses on the questionnaire?

Hillman discards the usual explanations of these phenomena. Psychology pioneer Alfred Adler had suggested that people achieve greatness to compensate for their inadequacies, but this does not begin to account for most of the remarkable cases of calling that Hillman describes.

Some psychologists attribute the sense of calling to parental influence, but Hillman argues that the call to greatness is often in spite of parental pressures. For example, Igor Stravinsky was chided by his mother for not following the example of more conventional musicians, like Scriabin. She did not hear her son's *Le Sacre du printemps,* one of the epoch-making compositions of the century, until its twenty-fifth-anniversary performance, a year before she died. Even then, she told friends that she would probably hate it, because it was not her kind of music.

My own mother didn't want me to become a rabbi, because she remembered that many rabbis in her native Europe had suffered indignities. A great career in the law would have moved me from relative poverty to wealth. She even suggested that accounting was a far better career for me than the rabbinate.

To be sure, some parents recognize their children's calling and nurture it. Van Cliburn's mother began to teach him piano when he was three, because he had already begun to play by ear a year earlier. His mother was wise and loving enough to help him on his path. But his calling was his own soul's code.

The movement from healing to wholeness begins with the search for one's calling, but discovering one's calling does not always require a career shift. It may simply permit one to broaden one's horizons by engaging in activities that make life more beautiful and uplifting. Do you remember Max's story? He did not need to change his career path when he discovered his calling as an empathic helper to patients with AIDS. A member of my congregation is a well-known endodontist in Beverly Hills. Dr. Rami Etessami told me that his life had been changed by one inspirational lecture. The speaker had invited members of the audience to follow their impossible dream. Rami's lifelong dream was to play the violin, but he suffers from hearing loss. As a child in Iran, two of that country's best-known violin teachers had tried to teach him, but said he lacked the basic auditory skills. In addition, reading music filled him with anxiety. And so Rami had believed that his dream could never be fulfilled—that is, until he accepted the lecturer's challenge. Then he purchased a violin and found a patient teacher. Lessons and practice sessions were extremely difficult, but he held on to his dream, and when he began to make music, he finally achieved his impossible dream. The first piece of music he performed successfully was Israel's national anthem, "Hatikvah"— the hope. His soul's calling had not interfered with his successful professional practice, but it had changed his life.

Every Tuesday morning I study the Zohar with Professor Kenneth N. Klee. Ken, an attorney specializing in bankruptcy law, had taught at Harvard, and then became a professor at the UCLA

School of Law. He was for many years plagued with chronic, unyielding physical pain. Eventually, he consulted a Reiki specialist. Her hands made no contact with his body, but their radiant energy was tangible. The pain disappeared and never returned. Ken's healing encounter was transformative, because he realized he'd been introduced to a new, powerful, nonphysical dimension. He enrolled for training as a radiance Reiki therapist, quickly discovering his own healing powers. He soon mastered a number of other healing modalities, became a regular meditator, and discovered that he had highly developed psychic abilities. He intuitively felt the need to discover the energies embedded in Jewish spiritual practice. His regular study of Kabbalah was the result of this process of spiritual discovery. Ken Klee did not leave the law. The establishment of the Klee Healing Ministry, and his increasing involvement with Kabbalah, are adjuncts to what he does for a living.

In more than forty years as a pulpit rabbi, my life has intersected with the lives of thousands of people. I've witnessed the life-changing effects of the newly discovered joys of studying sacred texts, and seen the transformative nature of active involvement in community welfare projects and social activism. I've delighted in the pleasure taken by hard-nosed businessmen in running youth groups and teaching classes in the religious school. I've been inspired by the music made by lawyers, professors, and tradespeople in our congregational choirs. All these people were busy making a living and raising their families, but had taken the time to smell the roses and answer a call that would further enrich their lives and the lives of those who knew them. They'd also discovered something important about who they really were.

Some people are lucky enough to discover their calling effortlessly. In most cases, the journey of discovery requires the investment of personal effort. The two best ways I know are prayer and meditation. People have told me they think it's wrong to bother God with their personal concerns, since, in the larger picture, these concerns must be rather trivial and the requests egoistic. I disagree. Our soul's code carries the divine imprint. God wants us to find happiness and add dimensions to our lives that will help us grow. The prayer book is designed to provide space for the expression of personal needs and concerns. Don't be embarrassed to ask God for help.

Throughout this book, I have emphasized the importance of regular meditation. As you develop your ability to move into the theta state, you will open yourself more and more to divine inspiration through your *Chochmah,* your most direct access to discovery and creativity. Before you meditate, ask God for help in finding your calling. You will not always be granted clear insight, but learn to trust your gut. The gut feeling you'll have, perhaps after many weeks and months of meditation, will be the opening for which you've asked. Don't be afraid. Test your intuitions by trying out what you think you're hearing. This will put you on your path. And do not forget to thank God for his blessings and help.

SPIRITUAL GROWTH THROUGH MEDITATION

Meditation can help ignite the spark of godness that sometimes burns dimly at the core of your being. It can grant you access to infinite knowledge and well-being. Because your soul is part of God, it has unimaginable potential.

Most of us are not conscious of the Divine within us. We've surrounded it with *kelipot* of darkness and doubt, and have surrendered to the appetites and passions of our *Nefesh.* But the spark has never been extinguished. It can be reignited and grow to fill our entire being with its light and energy.

Meditation is one of the ignition mechanisms God has granted us. Set aside twenty minutes a day, preferably in the morning, when you are not tired. Practice the meditations I have included here and in my CD. Read Rabbi Aryeh Kaplan's books on Jewish meditation. Use the techniques that resonate with your own soul. Try mantra meditations. The ones that work best for me are "*A-donai echad* [God is One]," "*Havayah,*" and "*Ehyeh.*" Recite your mantra silently over and over. Be completely attentive to the sound of the words, and if a thought distracts you, put it in a balloon and watch it float away, all the while continuing with your recitation. The purpose of the mantra is to quiet the static in your mind. Most of us are unaware that our minds are always active. Have you ever tried to keep your mind blank? Theoretically, you should be able to perceive nothing but emptiness, but this does not happen. Image after image will flicker across the video screen of your mind. There is so much static, so much "noise." By concentrating on the sound of one or two words, or even a bar of music, repeated over and over, the static diminishes, and the mind, your *Binah,* is suspended. But your *Chochmah* remains receptive, and the antennae of your *Neshamah* extended. You are open to inspiration from above and enlightenment from within.

I've used two techniques that have been particularly effective in enhancing my mantra meditation experiences. After reciting the mantra for ten or fifteen minutes, and clearing my mind, I imagine myself floating above my body, visualizing myself this way for a short time. I then envision my disembodied self expanding more and more until it fills the room and beyond, gradually becoming one with everything that exists as I become less and less conscious of my separate identity. Alternatively, after picturing myself out of body, I visualize my disembodied self beginning to spin, slowly at first, but with increasing speed, contracting as it moves rapidly in a vortex through my body into the innermost recesses of my soul, joining me to the Infinite within.

Meditation requires commitment and persistence, and the spiritual payoff is not immediate. But with practice, you will become more aware of your connection to *Havayah* and your soul will heal and grow.

SPIRITUAL GROWTH THROUGH PRAYER

Prayer is one of our least understood spiritual experiences. Most people ask God to grant their special and general needs. This notion of prayer derives from the Latin root *precari,* meaning "obtained by entreaty," but supplication is only part of the prayer experience.

Because we are created in the image of God, we often imagine that like God, we are completely independent. We exult in our ability to put men on the moon, conquer disease, and so on. Given enough time, we believe we can accomplish anything we wish. Yet, in a moment, everything can change. We're reduced to terrified impotence by the news that cancer cells are multiplying wildly in our bodies or by the sudden agonizing pain of a heart attack.

The Hebrew verb for *pray* is *le-hitpalel,* the reflexive form of the root *palal,* meaning "judge." Translated literally, the word *le-hitpalel* means "to judge yourself." Understood in this way, prayer is primarily self-judgment. When I pray, I judge myself vulnerable and in need. I stand before God, aware of the enormous disparity in our relationship. He is Being, Absolute and Infinite, while my being is contingent on my connection with him. He is autonomous, and I am wholly dependent. He is Creator, and I am merely creature. My sense of limitation, ephemerality, and dependence defines me as a prayer. I respond by trying to connect my *havayah* to Infinite *Havayah.* All prayer is the deepest expression of human yearning for the safety of attachment to *Havayah,* the divine Source.

In this context, prayer consciousness is worship. The original

English meaning of this word is enlightening. It derives from the word *worth-ship*. I turn to God in prayer both because I recognize his absolute and infinite worth, and also the contingent quality of my own worth. The initial gesture of prayer, therefore, is praise. This explains why the bulk of the Jewish prayer book consists of Psalms, the most inspired collection of praise of God in all of literature. The main prayer of the three daily services and the four festival services is called the *Amidah*. In rabbinic literature, this centerpiece of Jewish worship is simply called **tefillah**—the prayer. It consists of nineteen paragraphs, the first three of which express our praise of God. This is worth-ship in its classical sense. The thirteen intermediate paragraphs make specific and logically sequenced requests that are all articulated in the plural. The significance of the plural form is our recognition that we are all part of larger collectives—families, communities, societies, and nations. These prayers of supplication are meant to sensitize us to the needs of others. Abraham Joshua Heschel, one of the great religious thinkers of the twentieth century, commented that the printed supplications also respond to a profound personal need. Sometimes we need to be reminded about what we really need.

For centuries, many of the supplications in the *Amidah* prayer must have seemed absurd. Each paragraph of supplication concludes with a formula of blessing in the present tense, as if the petition were already granted. For example, the last of the paragraphs is a plea to God to hear our words. It concludes, "Blessed are you, O God, who hears prayer."

A number of the paragraphs deal with the condition of the Jewish people in exile from the Promised Land. One asks for the restoration of judges who will judge in accordance with Jewish law. That paragraph concludes, "Blessed are you, O God, who loves justice and righteousness." The next is a prayer for the defeat of evildoers and arrogant abusers of power. It concludes, "Blessed are you, O God, who crushes the enemy and subdues the arrogant." That is followed by a prayer for saints and sages. It concludes, "Blessed are you, O God, the staff and security of the righteous." It is followed by a prayer for the rebuilding of Jerusalem and the reestablishment of the throne of David, concluding, "Blessed are you, O God, who builds Jerusalem."

These supplications were recited three times a day during the two thousand years of exile. Countless generations prayed for justice yet suffered from manifest injustice and persecution, and prayed for the rebuilding of Jerusalem, which continued to remain desolate. Yet every prayer praised God as if the petitions had already been granted.

If these supplications had been simple wish lists at a heavenly supermarket, Jews would have stopped praying long ago. But they were not. They were the assertions of the faithful that God could and would intervene. The supplications were less a list of requests than a declaration of faith.

Appropriately, the final three blessings of the *Amidah* are an expression of gratitude. The faithful are grateful that the infinite God loves his finite creatures sufficiently to hear their pleas, even while preoccupied with maintaining the entire cosmos. That is faith. That is prayer.

Standardized prayer often seems a little contrived, because the words were composed by authors who lived in other circumstances at other times. How can we appropriate such prayers? Meaningful prayer requires **kavannah.** This word has been variously translated as "direction," "intentionality," "mindfulness," and "focus." Each of these translations captures something of its essence. The prayer should be focused on what he or she is saying, mindful of the sense of the words, aware of being in the presence of God, and intent on establishing a connection with the Divine.

The words of the prayer book are set. They are said in the same way by countless individuals and translated into many languages. But prayer with *kavannah* requires that these set words and sentences be given subjective meaning. No two people relate to God in exactly the same way. This is why the *Amidah* prayer opens with the formulation "God of our fathers, God of Abraham, God of Isaac, and God of Jacob." This could have been expressed in fewer words: "God of Abraham, Isaac, and Jacob." Why the repetition of the phrase "God of"? It teaches us that Abraham perceived God differently from Isaac, and that they each perceived God differently from Jacob. It could not have been otherwise. Even the same person relates to God differently at different times. We relate to him in one way when we are happy and successful, and in another when our hearts are broken and our hope has all but faded. Mindful prayer means pausing to reflect on how the prayer expresses your personal needs and your personal situation vis-à-vis God. When you become your prayer, it becomes your springboard to the Infinite.

Let me give you an example of this. The second paragraph of the *Amidah* reads as follows:

> You sustain the living in loving-kindness. You give life to the dead with great mercy. You support those who fall. You heal those who are sick. You release those who are bound. You remain faithful to those who sleep in the dust.

When I say these words mindfully, they take on special meaning. The phrase "You sustain the living" reminds me that my sustenance is a miracle and that I cannot take the food on my table for granted. My life is a gift, not a payoff for my good deeds. I cannot claim that I deserve God's grace. These musings, in turn, make me mindful of the power of *Chesed* and make me wonder whether I am loving enough to others, whether I'm as nonjudgmental of them as God is of me.

When I say the words "You give life to the dead," I sometimes think of those who meant so much to me and have passed on. I'm comforted by the thought that they are with me still. Sometimes I wonder whether I'm sufficiently aware that death will not be my final escape, and that I shall eventually have to account for the way I've lived my life.

When I say the words "You support those who fall," I can feel God's arm around my shoulder if I'm sad and depressed. When things go badly for me, I am comforted that God is there to catch me before I hit bottom. These words also inspired me to become a leader in the fight against apartheid in South Africa by becoming God's partner in supporting those whose lives and livelihoods had been crushed by that system.

I cannot but think of people who are sick when I say the words "You heal those who are sick," or of those who are stuck or trapped when I say the words "You release those who are bound." That phrase also gives me great hope and optimism when I find myself caught in a rut.

Kabbalistic masters used special **kavannot** when they pronounced the different names of God in their prayers, confident that their prayers would reverberate upwards through the Tree of Life, raising the divine energy higher and higher, and releasing new illuminations for their own souls. Rabbi Yechiel Barlev has published and explained these *kavannot* in his *Yedid Nefesh* edition of the prayer book of the Ari (Rabbi Isaac Luria), but unfortunately, this work has not yet been translated into English.

Formal Jewish prayer sometimes requires a spiritual dress code. Men and married women cover their heads at prayer. Men wear a

tallit (prayer shawl) at morning services, and, in addition, they don an aid called **tefillin** or phylacteries for weekday morning worship. Even these inanimate paraphernalia of prayer are conduits for divine energy.

Tefillin consist of two black leather boxes. One is strapped to the biceps, facing the heart, and the other is strapped on the head, high on the forehead between the eyes. The leather boxes house parchment inscribed with the four sections of the Torah that command us to "bind them [these words] as a sign upon your arms and as frontlets between your eyes" (Exod. 13:1–10, 13:11–16; Deut. 6:4–9, 11:13–21). The four passages are inscribed on a single piece of parchment in the leather box for the arm, and on four separate pieces in the box for the head, one for each of its four compartments. A long strap of leather is threaded through each of the boxes, and the leather strap of the box for the arm is knotted by the side of the box to resemble the Hebrew letter *yud*. The black leather strap of the tefillin for the head serves as a crown, and is knotted at the nape of the neck to form the letter *dalet*. The letter *shin* is embossed in two ways on the sides of the tefillin of the head. The three Hebrew letters formed by the two knots and the embossing make up the word ***Shaddai*,** meaning "Almighty [God]."

How do these boxes, parchment scrolls, and straps enhance our prayers? Why does God command us to put them on? Tefillin carry the energy of the Torah and are rich in symbolism. The tefillin for the head have separate scrolls, symbolizing the diversity of human approaches to prayer and God of which I have just written. The different scrolls represent different *kavannot,* subjective experiences, and ways of thinking about God. We perform actions with our arms, and righteous acts can be legislated and standardized. This is the function of the *Code of Jewish Law (Shulchan Arukh).* The *mitzvot* may carry different meanings for different people, but are performed in the same way by everyone who follows the *Code of Jewish Law.* Hence the single scroll in the tefillin for the arm. The tefillin are worn on the weaker of our arms, symbolizing the virtue of restraint, an aspect of *Gevurah.* The box faces the heart. The tefillin thus join head, hand, and heart to connect with the Infinite, embodying the commandment "And you shall love the Lord your God with all your heart, with all your soul, and with all your might" (Deut. 6:5). The leather strap of the tefillin is wound seven times around the forearm. It is then wound around the hand and fingers in such a way that the three Hebrew letters *shin, dalet,* and *yud* (*Shaddai*—Almighty) are formed. You will recall that this word is also formed by the knots of the tefillin and the embossing.

According to the Kabbalah, the tefillin have even deeper significance. The tefillin of the head represent the first three *Sefirot*—*Keter, Chochmah,* and *Binah.* The encircling strap is the crown, *Keter.* The box, which is aligned with the third eye, symbolizes our ability to receive inspiration through the three *Sefirot* of cognition: *Chochmah, Binah,* and *Da'at.* These are the *Sefirot* of the *Neshamah.* After the strap of the head tefillin has been knotted at the nape of the neck, it falls in two separate strands, one over each shoulder, symbolizing the two sides of the Tree of Life. The seven coils around the forearm represent the *Sefirot* of feeling, relating, and doing *(Chesed, Gevurah,* and *Tif'eret; Netzach, Hod,* and *Yesod;* and *Malchut),* which govern our being in the world.

I read an article in the newspaper *Forward* dated November 13, 2002, describing Dr. Steven Schram's personal experience with tefillin. Schram, a leading chiropractor and acupuncturist, had adopted Jewish religious practice not long before. While attending a conference in New York, he realized that the tefillin and their straps are placed on the major acupuncture channels. This occurred to him when the presenter was discussing the point in the nape of the neck and top of the spine where the channels converge. That is exactly where the tefillin of the head are knotted. Paying heed to his intuition, Schram investigated all the points of contact made by the tefillin and their straps. The diagrammed, footnoted version of his insight about the tefillin can be found in the October 2002 issue of the *Journal of Chinese Medicine* in his article "Tefillin: An Ancient Acupuncture Point Prescription for Mental Clarity." His main thesis is that the leather straps of tefillin, when worn properly, stimulate acupuncture points associated with improved concentration. My Kabbalah study buddy, Ken Klee, is a teacher of meditation in his spare time. He has told me that wearing tefillin during meditation has enhanced the quality of his own meditative experience.

Not all prayer is formalized. Indeed, when the recitation of the *Amidah* has concluded, we sit, resting our heads on our arms, and reach into the depths to connect with God. My great teacher, Rabbi Joseph B. Soloveitchik (the Rav), compared this type of (sometimes wordless) prayer to the howl of a wounded animal with its head between its legs. Our anguish and our pain is a connection with God more precious than any other. On one occasion, the sages sought to prevent an emotionally wounded colleague from addressing God in this way, fearful of the consequences to those who had hurt him (*B.T. Bava Metzia* 59b). This type of prayer is the model for all spontaneous prayer. It has no fixed times or requirements, and is simply the expression of the broken heart that God loves so much.

Meditative prayer is a powerful vehicle for the *Neshamah*. The prayers of Rabbi Nachman of Bratslav often rise to this level. They are the intimate conversations of creature and Creator, insulated from the noise and distraction of the world of sensation, perception, and conception. They are a wonderful way of achieving *hitbodedut,* seclusion with the Infinite.

MINDFUL LIVING: DEVELOPING
A SENSE OF WONDER

Rabbi Max Kadushin defined Jewish religious practice as "normal" mysticism. At first sight, his definition is difficult to understand, because the experience of connectedness with God seems far removed from mundane activities. However, closer examination shows that ordinary experiences can endow the normal with mystical significance. In the book on neurobiology to which I referred earlier, Andrew Newberg, Eugene D'Aquili, and Vince Rause write that all human beings are natural mystics, endowed with an inborn gift for effortless self-transcendence. People who have "lost" themselves in a beautiful piece of music or been swept away by a charismatic speaker have experienced the essence of mystical union in a small but revealing way. When people have fallen in love or been awestruck by the beauty of nature, they have experienced how it feels when the ego slips away for a moment or two. These magical moments are windows to that larger transcendent reality and unitary state that practiced mystics and meditators attain. The underlying neurobiological mechanism for transcendence links "the most profound experiences of the mystics with the smaller transcendent moments most of us experience every day" (*Why God Won't Go Away,* p. 115). In neurological terms, they differ only by degree.

Rabbi Abraham Joshua Heschel identifies common experiences of transcendence with the "sense of wonder," which can either be spontaneous or consciously developed through mindful living. Take eating for example. All living beings require nutrition to sustain themselves. Plants eat, animals eat, and humans eat. So how can eating become a springboard to the Infinite? The psalm-ist declared, "The earth is the Lord's and everything that is in it" (Ps. 24:1). In their comment on this verse, the sages point out that humans have no intrinsic right to anything, because everything belongs to God. But after blessing and thanking God for permit-ting us to benefit from his Creation, we take what we need for our-selves. The requirement to pause and recite a blessing before we eat puts a break on our desire and makes us become mindful of what we usually do mindlessly.

For instance, when I am about to eat an apple, I can take it in my hand and think about its delicate hues and wondrous pigmenta-tion, fascinated that apples come in so many different colors, sizes, shapes, and textures: some green, some yellow, some orange, with delicate hints of red and little streaks of pink; some large, some small; some round, some oval; some smooth, and some bumpy and rough. When I think this way, I'm delighted with my gift from its Creator. During this reverie, the apple ceases to be just another fruit, and I cannot but praise God. Then, still full of wonder, I take a bite, allowing myself to become aware of the juice on my tongue, of its sweetness or its tartness, as it brings my taste buds to life. Finally, with heightened awareness of its firmness or softness, I focus on the joys of chewing and swallowing.

Judaism sanctifies all our mundane activities. The bathroom is not usually associated with mindfulness. It is designed for the dis-posal of our bodily wastes, and most people do what they need to do and quickly return to their routines. Mindful living applies the brakes. After we have relieved ourselves and washed our hands, we pause to consider the miracle of a normally functioning human body, reflecting on its complex anatomy and physiology. We recite a blessing, giving thanks that the vessels that should be open are not blocked, and those that should be closed have not burst open.

Unfortunately, if we do not live mindfully, it takes a burst appendix, an enlarged prostate, or a twisted intestine to make us aware that "normal" bodily function is a miraculous gift, not to be taken for granted.

A rainbow in the sky can be viewed as a natural phenomenon, the refraction of light through moisture, but it can also inspire a sense of wonder when we contemplate the colors of the spectrum, their delicate nuances and subtle combinations. Normal mysticism transforms the refraction of light into an aesthetic delight to be celebrated with a blessing to the Lord of nature. It moves us to a higher level of consciousness, awakening our souls.

MYSTICISM AND ECOLOGICAL CONSCIOUSNESS

Heschel's notion of the sense of wonder also occurs in the religious philosophy of Rabbi Joseph B. Soloveitchik. Referring to the spiritually sensitive individual as *homo religiosus,* Rabbi Soloveitchik says: "He scans reality and is overcome with wonder, fixes his attention on the world, and is astonished" (*Halakhic Man,* p. 10). "The *homo religiosus* moves in a concrete world full of color and sound. He lives in his immediate, qualitative environment, not in a scientifically constructed cosmos" (*Halakhic Mind,* p. 40). Rabbi Soloveitchik's treatment of *homo religiosus* is perhaps most fully elaborated in his last, and arguably most important, philosophic work, *The Lonely Man of Faith,* which is based upon the contrasting descriptions of the creation of Adam and Eve in the first and second chapters of Genesis.

The Adam and Eve of the first chapter are portrayed as majestic, charismatic, creative, independent beings fashioned in the image of God, whose mandate is to "fill the world and conquer it"

(Gen. 1:28) and whose orientation is scientific and technological. In contrast, Adam and Eve in the second chapter are described as vulnerable, dependent, needy creatures, inspired with wonder by the grandeur of nature. Personifying the qualities of *homo religiosus,* their charge is to preserve and nurture their natural environment, "to cultivate it and to protect it" (Gen. 2:15). In this context, the garden of Eden represents the world, and protecting it means preserving it. The response of *homo religiosus* to his or her experience of wonder at God's creation is to become ecologically sensitive.

The cognitive gesture of *homo religiosus* is the attempt "to find in this concrete and physical world the traces of higher worlds, all of which are wholly good and eternal" (Soloveitchik, *Halakhic Man,* p. 13), or, stated in terms I have used earlier in the book, to find intimations of *Havayah* (Being) in the being of everything that exists in the natural world.

Because all of nature reflects divinity, the development of ecological consciousness is a legitimate expression of "normal" mysticism. Rabbi Moses Cordovero clearly implies this in *The Palm Tree of Deborah:*

> Furthermore, his mercy should extend to all creatures, neither destroying nor despising any of them. For the Supernal Wisdom *[Chochmah]* is extended to all created things—minerals, plants, animals and humans. This is the reason for the Rabbis warning us against despising food. In this way man's pity should be extended to all the works of the Blessed One, just as the Supernal Wisdom despises no created thing, for they are all created from that source . . . [The human being] should not uproot anything which grows, unless it is necessary, nor kill any living thing, unless it is necessary . . . To sum up, to have pity on all things and not to hurt them depends on Wisdom,

unless it be to elevate them higher and higher from plant to animal and from animal to human. For then it is permitted to uproot the plant and to kill the beast, to bring merit out of demerit. (pp. 83–85)

Expressed in these terms, ecological concern has consequences that transcend our normal experienced reality.

Ecological sensitivity is enshrined in religious laws. According to Maimonides, the biblical requirement for fields to lie fallow for twelve months every seven years is to preserve the earth and enhance its fertility (*Guide for the Perplexed*, 3:39). The Torah forbids the destruction of fruit trees for the production of battering rams during a siege (Deut. 20:19–20), but permits their destruction when they cause damage to other trees (*Mishneh Torah: Laws Governing Kings*, 6:8). Jewish reverence for nature is reflected in the talmudic opinion requiring scholars to pray for the recovery of a diseased tree (*B. T. Shabbat* 67a).

Concern for the ecology includes the prohibition against polluting the environment. Maimonides forbids any kind of activity that pollutes the air with dust particles that are harmful to the human habitat (*Mishneh Torah: Laws Governing Neighbors*, 11:1), and Rabbi Joseph Caro's authoritative *Shulchan Arukh (Code of Jewish Law)** extends this prohibition to all airborne contaminants (*Choshen Mishpat*, 155:22), as well as forbidding the pollution of the water supply (412:5).

Preservation of and concern for animals is high on the hierarchy of religious imperatives. The psalmist declares: "God is good to all

---

* Joseph Caro (1488–1575) is the author of the standard *Code of Jewish Law*. It is divided into four parts, two of which, *Choshen Mishpat (Juridical Procedures)* and *Yorehde'ah (Ritual Law)*, are referenced here. The first number identifies the chapter and the second the paragraph.

things and his mercy extends to all that he has made" (Ps. 145:9). Our animals must be fed before we feed ourselves (Deut. 11:15; *B. T. Gittin* 62a). Hunting for sport is explicitly forbidden (*Shulchan Arukh: Yoreh De'ah*, 23:4), and the slaughter of animals for food is governed by regulations whose purpose is to minimize pain and suffering (*Sefer ha-Chinukh*, p. 451). Sensitivity to the suffering of animals explains the scriptural imperative requiring the mother bird to be sent from the nest before her eggs are taken (Deut. 22:67). For the same reason, Jewish law forbids the simultaneous slaughter of the mother animal and its offspring (Lev. 22:28), and the cooking of the young animal in its mother's milk (Exod. 23:19, 34:26; Deut. 14:21). Farmers are forbidden to yoke animals of vastly different physical capacities together for such activities as plowing the land and pulling heavy equipment (Deut. 22:107).

Reverence for life is captured in the remarkable story (*B. T. Bava Metzi'a* 85a) about Rabbi Judah the Prince that I shared with you earlier. Punished for his insensitivity to the suffering of a young calf, he was healed only after he prevented the killing of rodents, declaring that "His tender mercies extend to all that he has made" (Ps. 145:9).

BEING THERE FOR OTHERS

Earlier, you learned that we are hardwired to be there for others. The *Sefirot* that govern our feelings, relationships, and actions are conduits for the passage of divine energy between us and other people. Open, balanced *Sefirot* enhance the flow of divine energy through our families, communities, and societies. Philosopher Emmanuel Levinas described authentic encounter with the other person as an "epiphany," a divine revelation. He held that our altruistic connection with the other is simultaneously an encounter with the Other. Levinas's view of the other person is not radically different from Franz Rosenzweig's notion of the other person as a commanding presence, calling us to responsibility and concern. Nor does it differ significantly from Martin Buber's view identifying the authentic I-thou relationship between two people with the I-Thou relationship of the individual and the Divine. Seen in this light, the way we interact with members of our families and others who need our help and support becomes as integral a part of our "normal" mystical experience as the strategies for mindful living I described in the last section.

Benevolence, altruistic and focused loving, active involvement in society, mindful living, regular prayer and meditation, being there for others, and helping preserve the ecology can all move us from healing to growth. When we begin to grow, there is no stopping us. The power within is infinite. We all have the tools to release and harness that energy to enlighten our lives and invest them with transcendent meaning.

AFTERWORD

The Kabbalah is an ancient tradition, encompassing a wide spectrum of knowledge. I have not attempted to present all, or even most, of what it has to offer. My focus has been the application of its principles to psychological dysfunction, healing, and spiritual growth.

The Kabbalah provides us with a unique model of functional and dysfunctional behavior. It suggests a method of diagnosis that accounts for all levels of human behavior and relationships. If this were all that we could learn from the Kabbalah about human nature and behavior, we would be more than satisfied, but it also allows us to move from diagnosis to healing and wholeness. I have described many kabbalistic healing and growth modalities and combined them with therapeutic strategies that have been proven to be effective in many clinical studies.

I hope that readers will be motivated to delve more deeply into the treasure house of this ancient Jewish mystical tradition. However, many of the primary sources are not yet available in English translation, and a good knowledge of Hebrew, Aramaic, and rabbinic literature is required to really understand authentic kabbalistic sources. Fortunately, there are a number of English versions of the Zohar. The Soncino Edition has been available for many years, and recently, the first two volumes of the Pritzker Edition, with translation and commentary by Daniel C. Matt, have appeared, and will be a useful guide to both scholars and laypeople. However, because the Zohar is an extraordinarily subtle and nuanced work that presumes prior knowledge of the major kabbalistic doctrines, it should, ideally, be studied only with a teacher who has that knowledge. Merely scanning its pages, as some have suggested, is fruitless. As a first step, I suggest solid, well-researched, and well-written introductory texts. For further reading in English, I recommend two excellent books without reservation—Rabbi Yechiel Barlev's *Song of the Soul: Introduction to Kaballa* (Petach-Tikva, 1994) and Rabbi Aryeh Kaplan's *Innerspace* (Jerusalem, 1991).

In the last few years, Kabbalah has become "hot." Well over a hundred works on Kabbalah were published in English in the years between 2001 and the middle of 2003. Some of these new books are doubtlessly of great value, but many others are New Age fluff. Check to make sure that books are authentic by inquiring into the rabbinic background and linguistic facility of their authors before you read them. A great tradition should not be sold short.

Self-help may sometimes not help. The diagnoses and interventions I've suggested may work for many people, but in others the problems may be deep-seated and may require intervention by a licensed mental health professional. Couples therapy and family therapy always require competent licensed therapists.

If the interventions in this book have not brought you substantial relief and healing, do not hesitate to consult a good therapist. I believe that psychological disorders are all sociopsychospiritual and that our spiritual deficits are as urgent as our psychological and sociological needs. So I advise you to select a licensed mental health professional who recognizes the importance of the spiritual dimension of human behavior and relationships. He or she will be able to take you to the next step of healing and growth.

According to an old rabbinic adage, one learns much more from one's students than from one's teachers. This book is the product of many hundreds of interactions with people who have attended my lectures on Kabbalah and psychology, my workshops, and my classes. They have all been my teachers. So have my clients. You have now also joined their ranks. Writing this book has been a personal growth experience for me. I thank you for your help, and, especially, the One who graces humankind with knowledge.

To Order the Meditation CD

The meditation CD, with embedded theta brain-wave pulses and music, may be obtained from the author for $18.00. For more information, please write to

Connecting to God
c/o Electric Indigo
8646 W. Pico Blvd.
Los Angeles, CA 90035

You may also call (310) 470-0080 or visit www.connectingtogod. com.

GLOSSARY

Acher Someone else; the designation for the apostate Rabbi Elisha ben Abuyah (second century C.E.), one of the four sages who delved deeply into the Jewish mystic tradition.

Alte Rebbe The (Venerable) Old Rabbi; the Yiddish designation for Rabbi Schneur Zalman of Lyadi (1745–1813), founder of Chabad Chasidism.

Amidah Standing prayer; the central part of the statutory Jewish prayer service, consisting of nineteen blessings, and recited standing, hence its name. It is also simply called *tefillah* (prayer).

Ari Acronym for *Elohi Rabbi Yitzchak* (The Divine[ly Inspired] Rabbi Isaac [Luria]; 1534–1572), the greatest of the kabbalistic masters.

Asiyah The universe of Doing; the last of the five principal kabbalistic parallel universes, our material visible universe; the realm of the last of the ten *Sefirot, Malchut.*

atarah Crown; also denotes the glans of the male sexual organ.

atbash Ancient Bible code in which the last letter of the Hebrew alphabet is substituted for the first, the second last for the second, and so on.

Atzilut The universe of Emanation; the second of the five principal parallel universes.

Ayin No-thingness; a designation for primordial existence that preceded Emanation and Creation.

Ayn Sof The Limitless One; the kabbalistic designation for Divinity.

Beriyah The universe of Creation; the third of the five principal parallel universes.

Binah Understanding, analytical intelligence; the designation of one of the *Sefirot* of cognition.

Chabad A Chasidic movement with worldwide outreach programs, founded by Rabbi Schneur Zalman of Lyadi (see **Alte Rebbe**).

ChaBaD Acronym for the three *Sefirot* of cognition: *Chochmah, Binah,* and *Da'at.*

ChaGaT Acronym for the three *Sefirot* of emotion: *Chesed, Gevurah,* and *Tif'eret.*

Chasidism Popular pietistic movement founded by Rabbi Israel Ba'al Shem Tov (1700–1760), deriving its inspiration from the Kabbalah, and consisting of a large number of groupings, each with its own customs; led, for the most part, by charismatic rabbis; often distinguishable by its dress code.

chaver Friend.

Chayah Living Essence; second-highest level of the human soul.

Chesed Loving-kindness; also called *Gedulah* (Greatness); the name of the first of the three *Sefirot* of emotion.

chevruta Study companion; individual with whom one dialogues about the meaning of a sacred text.

Chochmah Wisdom; also the name of the first of the three *Sefirot* of cognition.

Da'at Knowledge; also the name of the third of the three *Sefirot* of cognition.

derash Inquiry; the third of the four levels of biblical interpretation (see **PaRDeS**).

devekut Attachment to God; the goal of the Jewish mystic quest.

Din Judgment; also, an alternative name for the *Sefirah* of *Gevurah;* a designation for one of the three general types of Divine Providence.

Ehyeh I Shall Be; the divine name revealed to Moses at the burning bush.

Etz ha-Chayim The Tree of Life; the primary designation for the linear arrangement of the *Sefirot;* the blueprint of the cosmos; also, the title of the book summarizing Rabbi Isaac Luria's teachings, by his disciple Rabbi Chayim Vital.

gematria The numerical value of the letters of any given Hebrew word; an ancient Bible code.

Gevurah Power or restraint; the second of the three *Sefirot* of emotion; also called *Din.*

gilgul neshamot Reincarnation of souls; the mystic doctrine of the individual soul's many journeys on the path to perfection.

Havayah Being; designation for God as the Source of all being, and, particularly, as immanent in all beings.

Hilkhot Teshuvah The Laws of Repentance; part of Maimonides' codification of Jewish Law *(Mishneh Torah).*

hitbodedut Isolation; a term frequently used to describe the meditative experience.

Hod Majesty or empathy; the second of the three *Sefirot* of relationship.

Kabbalah The "received" mystical tradition of Judaism, originating with the revelation at Mount Sinai and developing through the ages; also, the collection of records of the Jewish mystical tradition.

kaddish Doxology; a second-century Aramaic prayer of praise; recited at the conclusion of each segment of the public worship service, and by mourners during the period of their bereavement and on the anniversary of bereavements (see *yahrzeit*).

kavannah Intentionality; mindfulness and focus in prayer and meditation.

kavannot Plural form of *kavannah;* also, kabbalistic incantations preceding prayer and the performance of other divine imperatives aimed at restoring the absolute unity of Divinity (see *tikkun*).

kedushah Holiness; also, the designation of a part of the *Amidah* prayer requiring a quorum of ten men.

kelipah (plural *kelipot*) Shard or shell; one of the remnants of the shattered vessels originally containing divine light, subsequently devoid of light and associated with evil and doubt.

kelipot noga The glowing shard or shell; the divine energy that glows within the negative energy of the shards; specifically, relating to those material things that are permitted and capable of transformation into holy energy through mindful intent.

Keter Crown; the highest of the *Sefirot;* repository of the Divine Will.

kibbud av The imperative to honor parents; the Fifth Commandment.

kiddushin Betrothal; a term derived from the Hebrew word *kedushah,* connoting holiness, reflecting the Jewish notion of the holiness of matrimonial union; also, a tractate of the Talmud that deals inter alia with marriage.

KoCHaB Acronym for the first three *Sefirot: Keter, Chochmah,* and *Binah.*

Ma'asei Bereishit The Works of Creation; a reference to the Creation chapters in Genesis; one of the major focuses of the Jewish mystical tradition.

Ma'asei Merkavah The Mystery of the Chariot; Ezekiel's vision (1:1–27; 2:1–2); the second primary focus of Jewish mystical contemplation; also, a key to the understanding of the dynamics of prophecy and meditation.

Malchut Sovereignty; the last of the ten *Sefirot;* associated with our material realm of *Asiyah,* and used, interchangeably, with the term *Shekhinah* (the feminine Divine Presence).

menatze'ach Conductor, director, conqueror; terms used in conjunction with the spiritual energies of the *Sefirah* of *Netzach.*

mezuzah Parchment scroll inscribed with the two paragraphs of the *Shema* prayer (Deut. 6:4–9; 11:13–20), affixed to the doorposts of one's home.

middot Virtues; specifically, a reference to the six *Sefirot* of emotion and relationship.

midrash Method of rabbinic Bible interpretation; also, the name given to the written record of rabbinic interpretations of the Bible.

Mi-she-bayrach A special supplication for healing, blessing, and protection; usually, but not exclusively, recited in the synagogue during the Torah reading service.

Mishnah The written record of the original exclusively oral Torah, edited by Rabbi Judah the Prince in ca. 200 C.E.; the basis of the Talmud.

mitzvah (plural *mitzvot*) Divine imperative; righteous deed; a reference to any of the 613 commandments of the Torah; also, a general designation for a good deed.

mochin Cognitive activities; a designation for the three *Sefirot* of cognition: *Chochmah, Binah,* and *Da'at.*

NaRaNCHaY Acronym for the five elements of the human soul: *Nefesh, Ru'ach, Neshamah, Chayah,* and *Yechidah.*

Nefesh The animal soul; the lowest of the five elements of the soul, responsible for our survival in our material environment.

NeHiY Acronym for the three *Sefirot* of relationship: *Netzach, Hod,* and *Yesod.*

Neshamah The element of the human soul responsible for thought processes; partly embodied and partly disembodied. The disembodied part of the *Neshamah* is our connection with the supernal worlds, and mediates inspiration, intuition, and creativity.

neshimah Breath.

Netzach Victory; the first of the three *Sefirot* of relationship; the spiritual root of focused interpersonal relationships.

olam katan Microcosm; the human being as a miniature version of supernal cosmic reality. Thus, knowledge of human nature and activity throws light on the supernal *Sefirot* of the Tree of Life.

Or demakifin Light that surrounds every individual; aura.

PaRDeS Acronym for the four methods of biblical interpretation—*peshat, remez, derash,* and *sod,* the latter three providing the basis for the Jewish mystic interpretation of Scriptures; also, a reference to the highest levels of the Jewish mystic experience; also, a term for Paradise, metaphorically referred to as *orchard.*

peshat The simple meaning of the text; the most superficial understanding of Scripture.

Pirkei Heichalot Rabati The Greater Book of the Divine Chambers, an ancient kabbalistic text ascribed to Rabbi Nechunia ben Ha-Kanah and his disciple, the High Priest Rabbi Yishmael ben Elisha (second century C.E.).

ReMaK The acronym for the great kabbalistic master, Rabbi Moses Cordovero (1522–1570).

remez Hint; Bible code used for scriptural interpretation; the second of the four methods of biblical interpretation (see **PaRDeS**).

Ru'ach Wind, spirit; the second element of the incarnated human soul, associated with emotions and relationships; the soul's interface with the realm of *Yetzirah* in deep meditation and prophecy.

Sefer Bahir The Book of Illumination, an early kabbalistic work ascribed to Rabbi Nechunia ben Ha-Kanah and his disciple, the High Priest Rabbi Yishmael ben Elisha (second century C.E.).

Sefer Yetzirah The Book of Formation, an early kabbalistic work that bears the stamp of Rabbi Akiva (50–135 C.E.).

Sefirah (plural *Sefirot*) Vessel for the divine energy, or filter, through which divine light and energy are refracted into their various components; the divine attributes. The Ten *Sefirot* are represented as the mystic Tree of Life, and are the spiritual roots or building blocks of the entire cosmos. They also account for human nature, cognition, emotion, relating, and doing.

Shaddai Almighty God.

Shekhinah The Divine Presence; the feminine aspect of Divinity that is associated with the realm of human corporeal and spiritual experience.

shibbud av Inappropriate control of children by parents.

sitra achra The other side, the Aramaic term for the domain of evil; the kabbalistic designation of evil forces that sustain themselves through leechlike attachment to human beings, following the inappropriate activities of the human animal soul and inappropriate human desires and relationships.

sitra de-kedushah The side of holiness; the opposite of *sitra achra.* The goal of human life is to transform the *sitra achra* into the *sitra de-kedushah.*

sod Secret; the deepest level of biblical interpretation; the kabbalistic interpretation of Scriptures; the last of the four levels of exegesis (see PaRDeS).

tallit Prayer shawl with four fringes, worn by men during morning worship.

Talmud The record of rabbinical discussions on biblical law and lore, consisting of the *Mishnah* and the *Gemara*. The version developed in the Holy Land (200–400 C.E.) is called the Jerusalem Talmud (JT). The version developed in Babylon (200–500 C.E.) is called the Babylonian Talmud (BT).

tefillah Prayer; specifically, a reference to the nineteen-blessing centerpiece of Jewish worship (see *Amidah*).

tefillin Phylacteries; two leather boxes containing parchment inscribed with the biblical imperative to "bind them [these words] as a sign upon your arm and as frontlets between your eyes" (Exod. 13:1–10, 13:11–16; Deut. 6:4–9, 11:13–21). One is worn on the arm and the other on the head by Jewish men during weekday morning worship. The boxes, as well as the straps with which they are attached to head, arms, and hand, have symbolic and mystical significance.

Tif'eret Glory, Splendor, Beauty; the third of the three *Sefirot* of emotion; also denoting the virtues of mercy and truth.

tikkun Repair, healing. The purpose of human existence is the repair of the cosmos through the elimination of evil and the performance of good deeds, prayer, meditation, and study; also, a reference to the repair of the *Sefirot* of the human soul; psychospiritual healing.

tikkunim Kabbalistically prescribed activities aimed at the repair of the individual and the cosmos.

tikkun olam Repair of the world or cosmos (see *tikkun*).

Tomchei Shabbos An organization that supplies Sabbath meals for the needy.

Torah The Five Books of Moses; the sacred teachings of Judaism.

Tzadik The righteous; rabbinic designation for the biblical Joseph; synonym for the *Sefirah* of *Yesod*.

tzimtzum The divine act of contraction that allowed space for the emanation of the cosmos from limitless Divinity *(Ayn Sof)*.

yahrzeit The anniversary of the passing of a loved one (see **kaddish**).

Yechidah Unification or unity; the highest level of the human soul; the closest association of the human soul with its Divine Source.

yesh Some-thing; a reference to the process of Creation, and the emergence of some-thing from its Divine Source, or No-thing (see *Ayin*).

yesh mi-Ayin Creation out of nothing; *creatio ex nihilo*.

yeshiva Academy of Jewish studies; originally the name given to institutions for advanced rabbinic studies, but now also the name for Orthodox Jewish day schools on the elementary and high school levels.

Yesod Foundation; the third of the *Sefirot* of relationship: *Netzach, Hod,* and *Yesod;* the spiritual root of the interface of supernal reality and human activity, concretized in the act of marital intimacy.

yetzer ha-ra The inclination to evil.

Yetzirah Formation; the fourth of the five principal parallel universes.

yizkor The memorial prayer for deceased relatives recited in synagogue on the three Pilgrim festivals (Passover, Shavuot, and Sukkot) and on Yom Kippur (the Day of Atonement).

Zohar *The Book of Splendor;* originally formulated orally by Rabbi Shimon bar Yochai (ca. 135 c.e.) and finally redacted by Rabbi Moses de Leon in the thirteenth century; the central work of the kabbalistic library; the mystical interpretation of the Torah.

BIBLIOGRAPHY

American Psychiatric Association. *Diagnostic and Statistical Manual of Mental Disorders.* Washington, D.C.: American Psychiatric Association, 1994.

Barlev, Yechiel. *Song of the Soul: Introduction to Kaballa.* Petach-Tikva, Israel: privately printed, 1994.

————. *Siddur Yedid Nefesh* [Prayer Book of the Ari]. Petach-Tikva, Israel: privately printed, 1999.

Beck, Aaron T., A. John Rush, Brian F. Shaw, and Gary Emery. *Cognitive Therapy of Depression.* New York: Guilford Press, 1979.

Beck, Aaron T., and M. Weishaar. "Cognitive Therapy." In *Comprehensive Handbook of Cognitive Therapy,* edited by Arthur Freeman, Karen M. Simon, Larry E. Beutler, and Hal Arkowitz, pp. 21–36. New York: Plenum Press, 1989.

Becvar, Dorothy S. *Soul Healing: A Spiritual Orientation in Counseling and Therapy.* New York: Basic Books, 1997.

Ben HaKanah, Nechunya. *The Bahir: Illumination.* With translation, introduction, and commentary by Aryeh Kaplan. York Beach, Maine: Samuel Weiser, 1989.

————. *Sefer ha-Bahir [The Book of Illumination].* Edited by Daniel Abrams. Los Angeles: Cherub Publications, 1994.

Blake Lucas, Winafred, ed. *Regression Therapy: A Handbook for Professionals.* 2 vols. Visalia, Calif.: Deep Forest Press, 1993.

Bloechl, Jeffrey, ed. *The Face of the Other and the Trace of God: Essays on the Philosophy of Emmanuel Levinas.* Perspectives in Continental Philosophy, no. 10. New York: Fordham University Press, 2000.

Bloomstein, Yolande. "The Soulmate Experience: A Phenomenological Investigation." Ph.D. diss., Pacifica Graduate Institute, 2000.

Buber, Martin. *I and Thou.* With translation, prologue, and notes by Walter Kaufmann. New York: Free Press, 1971.

Burns, David D. *The Feeling Good Handbook: Using the New Mood Therapy in Everyday Life.* New York: HarperCollins, 1989.

Burns, David D., and Aaron T. Beck. *Feeling Good: The New Mood Therapy.* New York: William Morrow, 1980.

Caro, Joseph. *Shulchan Arukh [Code of Jewish Law].* New York: Otzar Halakhah, 1965.

Cole, K. C. "A New Slice on Physics: Theory Alters Physics' Big Picture." *Los Angeles Times,* May 17, 2003.

Cordovero, Moses. *The Palm Tree of Deborah.* With translation, introduction, and notes by Louis Jacobs. London: Vallentine, Mitchell, 1960.

Dossey, Larry. *Healing Words: The Power of Prayer and the Practice of Medicine.* San Francisco: HarperSanFrancisco, 1993.

Dusay, John M., and Katherine M. Dusay. "Transactional Analysis." In *Current Psychotherapies,* edited by Raymond J. Corsini and Danny Wedding, pp. 405–453. Itasca, Ill.: Peacock, 1979.

Emrick, Chad D. "Alcoholics Anonymous and Other Twelve-Step Programs." In *Textbook of Substance Abuse Treatment,* edited by Marc Galanter and Herbert D. Kleber, pp. 351–358. Washington, D.C.: American Psychological Association Press, 1994.

Fanning, Patrick. *Visualization for Change.* Oakland, Calif.: New Harbinger, 1988.

Feinstein, David, and Stanley Krippner. *The Mythic Path: Discovering the Guiding Stories of Your Past—Creating a Vision for Your Future.* New York: G. P. Putnam's Sons, 1997.

Feldman, Aharon. *The River, the Kettle and the Bird: A Torah Guide to Successful Marriage.* Jerusalem: Feldheim, 1987.

Feldman, David M. *Marital Relations, Birth Control and Abortion in Jewish Law.* New York: Schocken Books, 1974.

Finkelstein, Adrian. *Your Past Lives and the Healing Process: A Psychiatrist Looks at Reincarnation and Spiritual Healing.* Farmingdale, N.Y.: Coleman Publishing, 1985.

Freeman, Arthur, Karen M. Simon, Larry E. Beutler, and Hal Arkowitz, eds. *Comprehensive Handbook of Cognitive Therapy.* New York: Plenum Press, 1989.

Freud, Sigmund. *The Future of an Illusion, Civilization and Its Discontents, and Other Works.* Translated and edited by James Strachey. London: Hogarth Press, 1961.

Gikatilla, Joseph. *The Holy Letter.* Translated and with an introduction by Seymour J. Cohen. Northvale, N.J.: Jason Aronson, 1993.

Goldberg, Bruce. *The Search for Grace: A Documented Case of Murder and Reincarnation.* Sedona, Ariz.: In Print Publishing, 1994.

Goldenberg, Irene, and Herbert Goldenberg. *Family Therapy: An Overview.* Pacific Grove, Calif.: Brooks/Cole Publishing, 2003.

Goleman, Daniel. *Emotional Intelligence: Why It Can Matter More Than IQ.* New York: Bantam Books, 1995.

———. *Destructive Emotions: How Can We Overcome Them? A Scientific Dialogue with the Dalai Lama.* New York: Bantam Dell, 2003.

Green, Elmer, and Alyce Green. *Beyond Biofeedback.* New York: Delacorte Press/S. Lawrence, 1977.

Greyson, Bruce. "Near-Death Experiences." In *Varieties of Anomalous Experience: Examining the Scientific Evidence,* edited by Etzel Cardeña, Steven J. Lynn, and Stanley C. Krippner, pp. 315–352. Washington, D.C.: American Psychological Association Press, 2000.

Grof, Christina. *The Thirst for Wholeness: Attachment, Addiction, and the Spiritual Path.* New York: HarperCollins, 1993.

Grof, Stanislav, and Christina Grof, eds. *Spiritual Emergency: When Personal Transformation Becomes a Crisis.* Los Angeles: Jeremy P. Tarcher/Putnam, 1989.

Halevi, Aaron. *Sefer ha-Chinukh* [The Book of Instruction]. Edited and with commentary by Charles B. Chavel. Jerusalem: Mosad Ha-Rav Kook, 1956.

———. *Sefer ha-Hinnuch* [The Book of Mitzvah Education]. Translated and with notes by Charles Wengrov. Student Edition. 5 vols. New York: Feldheim, 1978–1989.

Heschel, Abraham Joshua. *God in Search of Man: A Philosophy of Judaism.* New York: Farrar, Straus & Giroux, 1976.

———. *I Asked for Wonder: A Spiritual Anthology.* Edited by Samuel H. Dresner. New York: Crossroad, 1983.

Hillman, James. *The Soul's Code: In Search of Character and Calling.* New York: Random House, 1996.

Hirsch, W. *Rabbinic Psychology.* London: Edward Goldston, 1947.

Hunter, Marlene E. *Creative Scripts for Hypnotherapy.* New York: Brunner/Mazel, 1994.

Kadushin, Max. *Organic Thinking: A Study in Rabbinic Thought.* New York: Jewish Theological Seminary of America, 1938.

———. *The Rabbinic Mind.* New York: Bloch, 1972.

Kaplan, Aryeh. *Meditation and the Bible.* York Beach, Maine: Samuel Weiser, 1978.

————. *Meditation and Kabbalah.* York Beach, Maine: Samuel Weiser, 1982.

————. *Jewish Meditation: A Practical Guide.* New York: Schocken Books, 1985.

————. *Innerspace: Introduction to Kabbalah, Meditation and Prophecy.* Jerusalem: Moznaim, 1991.

Kaplan, Helen Singer. *New Sex Therapy: Active Treatment of Sexual Dysfunctions.* New York: Brunner/Mazel, 1974.

————. *The Evaluation of Sexual Disorders: Psychological and Medical Aspects.* New York: Brunner/Mazel, 1983.

————. *The Illustrated Manual of Sex Therapy.* 2nd edition. New York: Brunner/Mazel, 1987.

Kelly, Eugene W., Jr. *Spirituality and Religion in Counseling and Psychotherapy: Diversity in Theory and Practice.* Alexandria, Va.: American Counseling Association, 1995.

Kübler-Ross, Elisabeth. *On Death and Dying.* New York: Macmillan, 1969.

Kuhn, Thomas S. *The Structure of Scientific Revolutions.* Chicago: University of Chicago Press, 1996.

Lamm, Norman. *A Hedge of Roses: Jewish Insights into Marriage and Married Life.* New York: Feldheim, 1966.

Levinas, Emmanuel. *Totality and Infinity: An Essay on Exteriority.* Philosophical Series. Translated by Alphonso Lingis. Pittsburgh: Duquesne University Press, 1969.

Luquet, Wade. *Short-Term Couples Therapy: The Imago Model in Action.* New York: Brunner/Mazel, 1996.

Maimonides, Moses. *Mishneh Torah* [Codification of Jewish Law]. Jerusalem: Pardes, 1949.

————. *Guide for the Perplexed.* With translation by Shlomo Pines. Chicago: University of Chicago Press, 1963.

Masters, John C., Thomas G. Burish, Steven D. Hollon, and David C. Rimm. *Behavior Therapy: Techniques and Empirical Findings.* New York: Harcourt Brace Jovanovich, 1987.

Midrash Rabbah. 2 vols. Jerusalem: Lewin-Epstein, 1960.

Midrash Rabbah. Translated and edited by Harry Freedman and Maurice Simon. 10 vols. London: Soncino Press, 1939.

Mills, Antonia, and Steven J. Lynn. "Past-life Experiences." In *Varieties of Anomalous Experience: Examining the Scientific Evidence,* edited by Etzel Cardeña, Steven J. Lynn, and Stanley C. Krippner, pp. 283–314. Washington, D.C.: American Psychological Association Press, 2000.

Moody, Raymond. *Life After Life: The Investigation of a Phenomenon—Survival of Bodily Death.* New York: Bantam, 1975.

Moore, Thomas. *Care of the Soul: A Guide for Cultivating Depth and Sacredness in Everyday Life.* New York: HarperCollins, 1992.

Moreno, Jacob Levy. *Psychodrama.* Vols. 1–3. Boston: Beacon House, 1946–1969.

Morse, Melvin L. *Closer to the Light: Learning from the Near-Death Experiences of Children.* New York: Villard, 1990.

Newberg, Andrew, Eugene D'Aquili, and Vince Rause. *Why God Won't Go Away: Brain Science and the Biology of Belief.* New York: Ballantine, 2001.

Peck, M. Scott. *The Road Less Traveled.* New York: Simon & Schuster, 1978.

Perls, Frederick S. *The Gestalt Approach and Eyewitness to Therapy.* Palo Alto, Calif.: Science & Behavior Books, 1973.

Ring, Kenneth. *Life at Death: A Scientific Investigation of the Near-Death Experience.* New York: Coward McCann, 1980.

———. *Heading Toward Omega: In Search of the Meaning of the Near-Death Experience.* New York: Morrow, 1984.

Ring, Kenneth, and Evelyn Elsaesser Valarino. *Lessons from the Light: What We Can Learn from the Near-Death Experience.* Portsmouth, N.H.: Moment Point Press, 1998.

Rosenzweig, Franz. *The Star of Redemption.* Translated by William W. Hallo. Boston: Beacon Press, 1971.

Schram, Steven B. "Tefillin: An Ancient Acupuncture Point Prescription for Mental Clarity." *Journal of Chinese Medicine,* no. 70 (October 2002).

Schucman, Helen, and William Thetford. *A Course in Miracles.* New York: Foundation for Inner Peace, 1975.

Schulz, Mona Lisa. *Awakening Intuition: Using Your Mind-Body Network for Insight and Healing.* New York: Harmony, 1998.

Sefer Yetzirah: The Book of Creation. With translation, introduction, and commentary by Aryeh Kaplan. York Beach, Maine: Weiser, 1990.

Seligman, Martin E. P. *Learned Optimism: How to Change Your Mind and Your Life.* New York: Alfred A. Knopf, 1990.

Shafranske, Edward P., ed. *Religion and the Clinical Practice of Psychology.* Washington, D.C.: American Psychological Association Press, 1996.

Shakespeare, William. *Hamlet.* Folger Shakespeare Library. Edited by Barbara Moway and Paul Werstine. New York: Washington Square Press, 2003.

Smith, Manuel J. *When I Say No, I Feel Guilty.* New York: Doubleday, 1975.

Soloveitchik, Joseph B. *Halakhic Man.* Philadelphia: Jewish Publication Society of America, 1983.

———. *Halakhic Mind.* New York: Free Press, 1986.

———. *The Lonely Man of Faith.* New York: Doubleday, 1992.

Spitz, Elie Kaplan. *Does the Soul Survive? A Jewish Journey to Belief in Afterlife, Past Lives & Living with a Purpose.* Woodstock, Vt.: Jewish Lights, 2002.

Stone, Hal, and Sidra Winkelman. *Embracing Our Selves: The Voice Dialogue Manual.* Novato, Calif.: New World Library, 1989.

Sutherland, Cherie. *Reborn in the Light.* New York: Bantam, 1995.

Sutphen, Dick, and Lauren Leigh Taylor. *Past Life Therapy in Action.* Malibu, Calif.: Valley of the Sun, 1983.

Talmud Bavli [The Babylonian Talmud (B.T.)]. 20 vols. Jerusalem: Pardes, 1958.

The Talmud. Translated and edited by Isidore Epstein. 20 vols. London: Soncino Press, 1936.

Thompson, Jeffrey. *Theta Meditation System.* 2 compact discs. San Diego: Relaxation, 1999.

Weiss, Abner. *Rabbis as Mental Health Professionals.* Lanham, N.Y.: University Press of America, 2000.

Weiss, Brian L. *Many Lives, Many Masters: The True Story of a Prominent Psychiatrist, His Young Patient, and the Past-Life Therapy That Changed Both Their Lives.* New York: Simon & Schuster, 1988.

———. *Mirrors of Time: Using Regression for Physical, Emotional, and Spiritual Healing.* Carlsbad, Calif.: Hay House, 2002.

Wilber, Ken. *A Brief History of Everything.* Boston: Shambhala, 1996.

Wolpe, Joseph. *The Practice of Behavior Therapy.* Boston: Allyn & Bacon, 1991.

Woolger, Roger J. *Other Lives, Other Selves: A Jungian Psychotherapist Discovers Past Lives.* New York: Doubleday, 1987.

Zohar. With translation and commentary by Daniel C. Matt. Pritzker Edition. 2 vols. Stanford, Calif.: Stanford University Press, 2004.

Zohar. With translation by Harry Sperling, Maurice Simon, and Paul P. Levertoff. Soncino Edition. 5 vols. London and New York: Soncino Press, 1933–1934.

Zohar. With Hebrew translation and commentary by Yechiel Barlev. 13 vols. Petach-Tikva, Israel: privately printed, 1996.

INDEX

Aaron, 116. See also *Hod*
Abraham, 101, 108, 271. See also
    Chesed
Absolute Being, 38
abuse, 123, 128, 153, 155
    sexual, 115–16, 227, 246–49
acceptance, as grief stage, 205
accurate empathy, 114
Acher, 27–28, 29. *See also* Ben
    Abuyah, Rabbi Elishah
Action, consequences of, 131–32,
    141, 197. See also *Asiyah*
acupuncture, 274–75
Adam and Eve
    as archetypes, 23
    creation of, 19, 35, 48–49,
        53–54, 278–79
    Da'at and, 96, 118, 120, 121
Adler, Alfred, 263
aesthetics, 125, 143, 171
affluenza, 147–48
air pollution, 280
Akiva, Rabbi, 24–25, 27, 28, 230.
    See also *Sefer Yetzirah*
Alcoholics Anonymous, 57
alpha brain waves, 184
Alte Rebbe. *See* Zalman, Rabbi
    Schneur
altruism, 120, 281–82
Amidah, 63–64, 269–70, 271, 275.
    See also prayer
angels, 41

anger, as grief stage, 204
animals, 43, 113, 195
    concern for, 280–81
    Nefesh and, 55
    ritual slaughter of, 16–17, 281
animal soul level. See *Nefesh*
antithesis, 107
anxiety, 105, 177
archetypes, 13, 23, 104, 108, 116
Archimedes, 84
    Arkowitz, Hal, 182
Asiyah (Action), 41–42, 43, 56, 62,
    129, 131, 134, 241, 244
Assagioli, Roberto, 13–14, 51
assertiveness training, 167,
    199–200, 203, 208–9, 213,
    227, 228
atarah, 122, 126
atbash code, 21
Atzilut (Emanation), 40, 43, 51–52,
    63, 133
authentic relationships, 123–26
authoritarianism, 142–43, 144
Avot, 17, 22, 104, 222, 241–42
awe, 105. See also *Gevurah*
Ayin (No-thingness), 38, 40, 43,
    51, 52, 77, 97, 133
Ayn Sof (Limitlessness), 38, 40, 73,
    75

Babylonian Talmud, 17n, 24
    Avot, 17, 22, 104, 222, 241–42

rebalancing *(cont'd)*
of *Malchut,* 241–53
of relating *Sefirot,* 217–40
wholeness and, 258
reclaiming of life, 156–70
achieving completion and,
164–70
examining life script and, 157–62
taking responsibility and, 162–64
redemption, 32
reeducation, 234–36
referrals, sex therapy, 236
regression
meditative, 145
past-life therapy, 12–13, 69–70,
145–46, 154–55
reincarnation, 12–13, 53, 63–72,
145–46
undoing past errors and, 154–55,
164
reinforcement schedules, 250–51,
253
relationships, 111–28
authentic, 123–26
Hod and, 111, 113–16, 122–23,
125, 127–28
Netzach and, 111–13, 121, 122,
125, 127–28
rebalancing of, 217–40
tefillin and, 274
Torah prohibitions, 56
Yesod and, 111, 116–24, 126,
127–28
relaxation, 209
religion. *See* spirituality
ReMaK. *See* Cordovero, Rabbi
Moses
remez, 20–22. *See also* Four Levels
of Torah
repairing. See *tikkun*
reparenting, 175–76, 199, 248
repentance, 180, 183, 196
reproduction, 55–56

rescripting, 229
responsibility, 98, 162–64, 168, 227
right brain, 86, 171, 187
Rimm, David C., 167, 179, 200
Ring, Kenneth, 67, 90
River, the Kettle and the Bird, The
(Feldman), 234
Rivlin, Rabbi Hillel, 31
role-play, 167, 176, 179–80, 203,
209, 213, 221, 227
Roman Empire, 24
Rosenszweig, Franz, 282
Ru'ach (Emotional soul function,
wind, spirit), 53, 54, 56–61,
62, 98, 110, 122, 127, 197

Sabbath. See *Shabbat*
sadness, 105
safar. See *Sefirot*
saints, 42
Samuel, 66
sapir. See *Sefirot*
Saul, 66, 120
schizophrenia, 28, 163–64
Scholem, Gershom G., 30
Schram, Steven, 274–75
Schulz, Mona Lisa, 86
Schweitzer, Albert, 125
scientific revolution, 31–32
script for living, 229
security, 104
seers, 42
sefar/sefer. See *Sefirot*
Sefer Bahir, 25
Sefer ha-Chinukh, 281
Sefer Yetzirah, 25
Sefirot, 38, 61, 73–133
as blueprint, 74–77, 100, 123–24
dark side of, 146–47, 155, 170
families and, 138–40, 281
imbalance and, 134, 137–39,
148–53, 155, 156, 170,
197–98, 201

ABOUT THE AUTHOR

ABNER WEISS studied for the rabbinate in his native South Africa and Israel. He has master's and Ph.D. degrees in Jewish philosophy from Yeshiva University in New York, a master's in psychology from California State University, and a Ph.D. in psychology from the Saybrook Graduate School and Research Center in San Francisco. He is a licensed marriage and family therapist, a clinical member of the American Association of Marriage and Family Therapists, and a member of the American Psychological Association. Dr. Weiss was senior rabbi of Durban, South Africa, the Riverdale Jewish Center in New York, Beth Jacob Congregation of Beverly Hills, and the Western Marble Arch Synagogue in London. He has held professorships in Jewish thought at the University of Natal, Yeshiva University, and the University of London. He has served as chief judge of the Rabbinical Court (Beth Din) of Los Angeles, president of the Board of Rabbis of Southern California, chairman of the North American Cabinet of the State of Israel Bonds, and vice president of the Rabbinical Council of America. Rabbi Weiss has studied the Kabbalah since 1965, and lectured and facilitated workshops on the Kabbalah in North America, South Africa, Australia, and the United Kingdom. He lives in Los Angeles with his wife, Dr. Yolande Bloomstein, and is rabbi of the Westwood Village Synagogue and copresident of Village Mental Health Associates.

A Note on the Type

This book was set in Adobe Garamond, a typeface designed by Robert Slimbach in 1989. It is based on Claude Garamond's sixteenth-century type samples found at the Plantin-Moretus Museum in Antwerp, Belgium.